A Police Organizational Model for Crime Reduction:

Institutionalizing Problem Solving, Analysis, and Accountability

By

Rachel Boba, Ph.D.
Associate Professor
Florida Atlantic University

Roberto Santos, MS
Detective Lieutenant
Port St. Lucie, FL Police Department

A Police Organizational Model for Crime Reduction:

Institutionalizing Problem Solving, Analysis, and Accountability

By

Rachel Boba, Ph.D.
Associate Professor
Florida Atlantic University

Roberto Santos, MS
Detective Lieutenant
Port St. Lucie, FL Police Department

This project was supported by Cooperative Agreement #2007-CK-WX-K007 awarded by the Office of Community Oriented Policing Services, U.S. Department of Justice. The opinions contained herein are those of the author(s) and do not necessarily represent the official position or policies of the U.S. Department of Justice. References to specific agencies, companies, products, or services should not be considered an endorsement by the author(s) or the U.S. Department of Justice. Rather, the references are illustrations to supplement discussion of the issues.

The Internet references cited in this publication were valid as of the date of this publication. Given that URLs and websites are in constant flux, neither the author(s) nor the COPS Office can vouch for their current validity.

September 2011

Table of Contents

List of Figures

List of Tables

Dear Colleagues,

For over 30 years, researchers have evaluated the effectiveness of police crime reduction strategies and have shown that the strategies that are focused and data-driven are most effective. Approaches such as community policing, problem-oriented policing, hotspots policing, Compstat, and more recently, predictive and intelligence-led policing, are centered on using data and analysis to guide police in these efforts. However, there has been a gap in fully institutionalizing any one of these approaches into the everyday operations of police departments.

With support from the COPS Office, Dr. Rachel Boba and the Port St. Lucie, Florida Police Department have developed and implemented an organizational model for crime reduction that seeks to systematize problem solving, analysis, and accountability so that they become institutionalized into what police do. The model has also been enhanced and improved through its implementation in a range of police agencies across the United States as well as through focus groups with police researchers and practitioners at every level (e.g., commanders, supervisors, line level officers, and crime analysts). The purpose of the model is to take the results of research on police effectiveness and provide a structure to implement effective crime reduction approaches in a systematic way that can be modified for a specific agency based on its size, organizational structure, resources, and crime problems.

Thus, police leaders seeking to improve the efficiency, effectiveness, and accountability of their agency's current crime reduction efforts and to implement new strategies will find this report informative and instructive. It clearly outlines the model, its assumptions, and its practical implementation by describing the best use of problem solving and providing illustrations of actionable crime analysis products.

My hope is that this publication serves as a tool for taking decades of research of police effectiveness in crime reduction and translating the results into a practical organizational model that can be tailored and adapted to any individual police agency to improve and systemize their crime reduction efforts.

Sincerely,

Bernard K. Melekian, Director

Office of Community Oriented Policing Services

About the COPS Office

THE OFFICE OF COMMUNITY ORIENTED POLICING SERVICES (THE COPS OFFICE) is the component of the U.S. Department of Justice responsible for advancing the practice of community policing by the nation's state, local, and tribal law enforcement agencies through information and grant resources. The community policing philosophy promotes organizational strategies that support the systematic use of partnerships and problem-solving techniques to proactively address the immediate conditions that give rise to public safety issues such as crime, social disorder, and fear of crime. In its simplest form, community policing is about building relationships and solving problems.

The COPS Office awards grants to state, local, and tribal law enforcement agencies to hire and train community policing professionals, acquire and deploy cutting-edge crime-fighting technologies, and develop and test innovative policing strategies. The COPS Office funding also provides training and technical assistance to community members and local government leaders and all levels of law enforcement.

Since 1994, the COPS Office has invested more than $16 billion to add community policing officers to the nation's streets, enhance crime fighting technology, support crime prevention initiatives, and provide training and technical assistance to help advance community policing. More than 500,000 law enforcement personnel, community members, and government leaders have been trained through COPS Office-funded training organizations.

The COPS Office has produced more than 1,000 information products—and distributed more than 2 million publications—including Problem Oriented Policing Guides, Grant Owners Manuals, fact sheets, best practices, and curricula. And in 2010, the COPS Office participated in 45 law enforcement and public-safety conferences in 25 states in order to maximize the exposure and distribution of these knowledge products. More than 500 of those products, along with other products covering a wide area of community policing topics—from school and campus safety to gang violence—are currently available, at no cost, through its online Resource Information Center at www.cops.usdoj.gov. More than 2 million copies have been downloaded in FY2010 alone. The easy to navigate and up to date website is also the grant application portal, providing access to online application forms.

Acknowledgments

We are most grateful to the Port St. Lucie, Florida Police Department for valuing research, embracing new ideas, and implementing this model into its organizational structure. In particular, we would like to express our gratitude to the former chief of police John Skinner, for initiating and leading the partnership for five years, and former chief of police Donald Shinnamon, for continuing the partnership and enhancing the model's implementation through 2010. We would also like to acknowledge the former assistant chief and now current Chief Brian Reuther for his contributions and consistent support of the work over the last seven years, as well as Michelle Chitolie and Cheryl Davis, the department's outstanding crime analysts and two of the best in the country.

We would like to thank the Office of Community Oriented Policing Services (the COPS Office) for funding the grant that initiated this project in 2003, as well as the second grant in 2007 that facilitated the evaluation of the model and publication of this guidebook. In particular, we recognize Matthew Scheider and Nicole Scalisi for their support as well as their contribution to the ideas presented in the guidebook, and also the COPS peer reviewers for their thoughtful comments. We would also like to thank the following practitioners and academics who participated in two focus groups in May 2008 and April 2009, respectively, as part of this project. The goal of the focus groups was to critique and enhance the practical relevance and theoretical foundation of the Stratified Model. The participants included:

Major John Diggs and Mike Humphrey (Crime Analyst), Charlotte-Mecklenburg, NC PD

Major Tom Ryan and Glenn Duncan (Crime Analysis Manager), Fairfax County, VA PD

Captain Frank Amandro and April Lee (Crime Analyst), Fort Pierce, FL PD

Lieutenant Art Adkins and Erika Jackson (Crime Analyst), Gainesville, FL PD

Chief John Skinner, Chief Bryan Reuther, Michelle Chitolie (Crime Analyst), and Cheryl Davis (Crime Analyst), Port St. Lucie, FL PD

Dr. John Crank, Professor, University of Nebraska, Omaha

Dr. Robert Langworthy, Professor, University of Central Florida

Michael Scott, Director, Center for Problem-Oriented Policing

Dr. Ellen Scrivner, Director, John Jay Leadership Academy, NY

Dr. David Weisburd, Professor, George Mason University, VA

Lastly, we thank the following police agencies around the world that have participated in the improvement of the model through training and discussions, and/or have implemented the model themselves, and have shared with us the challenges they have faced as well as the successes they have had:

Anne Arundel County, MD Police Department

Champaign, IL Police Department

Cincinnati, OH Police Department

Dayton, OH Police Department

Fairfax County, VA Police Department

Fort Pierce, FL Police Department

New Zealand National Police

Royal Canadian Mounted Police (Langley, British Columbia)

Introduction

This guidebook presents a new and comprehensive organizational model for the institutionalization of effective crime reduction strategies into police agencies, called the *Stratified Model of Problem Solving, Analysis, and Accountability* (i.e., "Stratified Model"), along with the specific mechanisms, practices, and products necessary to carry out the approach in any police agency, no matter the size or the crime and disorder levels. Consequently, the purpose of the guidebook is to present the Stratified Model in a succinct and practical way in order to provide direction for institutionalizing effective crime reduction strategies and accountability. The goal is to discuss the applicability of the problem solving process and accountability procedures as well as present relevant analytical products that can immediately be used to systematically implement crime reduction strategies.

Although any police leader will find this guide informative, it is mainly written for police managers and commanders who are seeking to improve the efficiency, effectiveness, and accountability of their agency's crime reduction efforts. It will also be most useful to those with an understanding of basic organizational change and leadership principles and methods. This guidebook is not a primer to police leadership nor does it provide instruction on how to enact organizational change in a police agency. It simply presents an effective model that can be used as a template for

systematizing crime reduction strategies, analysis products, and accountability processes. A model based on the assumptions that problem solving is an effective process for addressing simple and complex problems, that crime reduction strategies can and should be guided by analysis, and that an accountability structure is imperative for enacting and sustaining change in a police agency.

The guidebook first presents the foundations and elements of the Stratified Model, then provides guidelines for implementing crime reduction strategies at different levels and evaluation of these efforts, as well as an organizational structure of accountability. Although the objective is to implement all aspects of the Stratified Model, an agency may choose to implement parts of the model as appropriate or to implement the model in phases. As a result, the guidebook provides a separate discussion of how problem solving, analysis, and accountability occur at each level of crime reduction—immediate, short-term, and long-term—that is followed by a discussion of evaluation and an organizational structure of accountability that would be used if all levels of crime reduction are implemented simultaneously. At the end of the guide, the information is synthesized into a table illustrating a framework that can be easily adapted for agencies that seek to tailor the model and implement it into their own organizational structure.

Foundations in Practiced-Based Research

There is a growing body of research that suggests that problem-oriented policing combined with problem solving can lead to more effective control and prevention of crime and disorder.[1] Yet, a number of scholars have recognized that use of the problem solving process in police agencies is often unsophisticated and relies heavily on the line-level officer's initiative to be conducted.[2] Isolated examples of innovative approaches to the process of scanning, analysis, response, and assessment that scholars have proposed can be found in police organizations, but systematic implementation of crime reduction strategies at levels beyond answering calls for service and investigating crimes are difficult, if not impossible, to find.[3]

CompStat, an innovative crime reduction approach recently adopted in many police agencies in the United States and around the world, is an attempt to synthesize an accountability structure and a strategic problem solving approach. Ideally, police commanders are supposed to be held accountable for both knowing about problems and doing something about the problematic activity in regular scheduled meetings.[4] However, in practice, CompStat's systematic model is not complete in its organizational implementation—often being driven by simple maps of crime to identify "hotspots" and by accountability meetings attended primarily by the highest ranks that are typically focused only on incident suppression or short-term strategies.[5]

The *Stratified Model of Problem Solving, Analysis, and Accountability* created and refined by Dr. Rachel Boba and Detective Lieutenant Roberto Santos is an approach to crime reduction that seeks to overcome the weaknesses of current policing methods, while at the same time incorporates the best practices of problem-oriented policing, CompStat, hotspots policing, traditional policing, and other models of policing, such as disorder policing and intelligence-led policing. The Stratified Model and its structure, processes, and products are the result of "practice-based"[6] research (i.e., applied research) conducted by the authors over the last seven years while implementing the Stratified Model into the Port St. Lucie, Florida Police Department (PSLPD)[7] through two COPS Office grants, as well

as in other agencies around the United States.[8] Notably in 2008, the PSLPD received the inaugural *Excellence in Law Enforcement Research Award* from the International Association of Chiefs of Police (IACP) for its collaborative partnership with Dr. Boba and the implementation of the Stratified Model.[9]

The Stratified Model outlines a framework for institutionalizing crime reduction strategies into the police organization and its day-to-day practices by providing clear actionable crime analysis products and a foundation for holding personnel accountable for conducting problem solving through a structured set of meetings. It is centered on the variable scope of activity that is addressed—from short-term individual or groups of incidents to long-term more complex problems—and the requirement of stratified, but integrated, organizational crime reduction strategies and accountability. For the crime reduction activities to become institutionalized in a police organization, they must not be carried out by a specialist squad, assigned to the lower ranks, or addressed only as preparation or a result of a meeting, but must be an integral part of the organizational mission and the day-to-day operations. Thus, levels of activity (types of problems) are distinguished within the model, and responsibility for both problem solving and accountability is distributed across the rank structure, instead of assigned only to line officers, management level supervisors, or a designated unit. The types of problems addressed with these strategies are matched by the rank and level of resources available to analyze and respond to the problem. The goal of the Stratified Model is to institutionalize effective crime reduction strategies through the implementation of problem solving, analysis, and accountability processes at every level in a police agency to enhance and increase its overall efficiency and effectiveness in addressing crime and disorder.[10]

This guide contains a more detailed overview of the Stratified Model that is followed by discussion of the implementation of immediate, short-term, and long-term crime reduction strategies, evaluation of these strategies, and an organizational structure of accountability. Because the Stratified Model can be applied to any sized police agency with varying rank structures, the guide ends with a general framework for rank assignment for the Stratified Model that can be taken and adapted to an agency based on its size and organizational structure.

Stratified Model of Problem Solving, Analysis, and Accountability[11]

For effective crime reduction strategies to become institutionalized in a police organization, they must be an integral part of the organizational mission and operations. Thus, the Stratified Model is an approach through which problem solving, analysis, and accountability processes are infused into the *existing* organizational structure and daily business of a police agency—with the goal of enhancing and increasing effectiveness and efficiency of crime reduction efforts that may already be occurring, but less systematically and with sporadic accountability.

ability process, that the strategies are implemented and are effective. That is, by separating and distinguishing the types of problems, different analyses, crime reduction responses, and accountability are carried out by different personnel within the agency, which *stratifies* the workload and responsibility.

Importantly, responsibility for systematic problem solving is linearly related (illustrated by the lower line) to rank with higher ranking officers being responsible for more complex problems which require more in depth and complex responses. Systematic accountability is also linearly related to rank and is parallel to systematic problem solving (illustrated by the upper line). It is carried out through systematic assessment and evaluation, a routine tracking system of responses and their results, as well as regular meetings that correspond to the temporal nature of the activity they address.

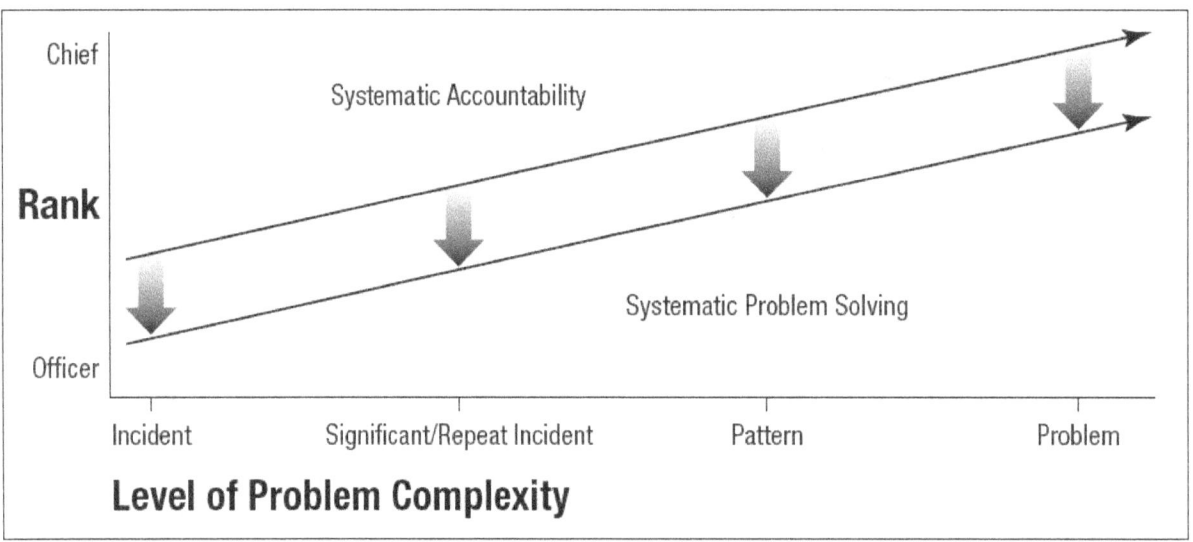

Figure 1: Stratified Model

Stratified Model Synopsis

The Stratified Model distinguishes among different types of problems for which crime reduction strategies are implemented, and assigns specific ranks with the responsibility for solving these problems. Figure 1 illustrates that more complex problems are assigned to higher ranks in the organization and that the traditional hierarchical structure of the police organization ensures, through an account-

Problem Solving Process

Importantly, the Stratified Model is not a form or version of Problem-Oriented Policing (POP), but seeks to take the effective elements of POP and integrate them with the effective elements of other crime reduction approaches (e.g., CompStat, hotspots policing). Thus, the Stratified Model is based on the assumption that the problem solving process (SARA) is effective and that *all* levels of problems—from

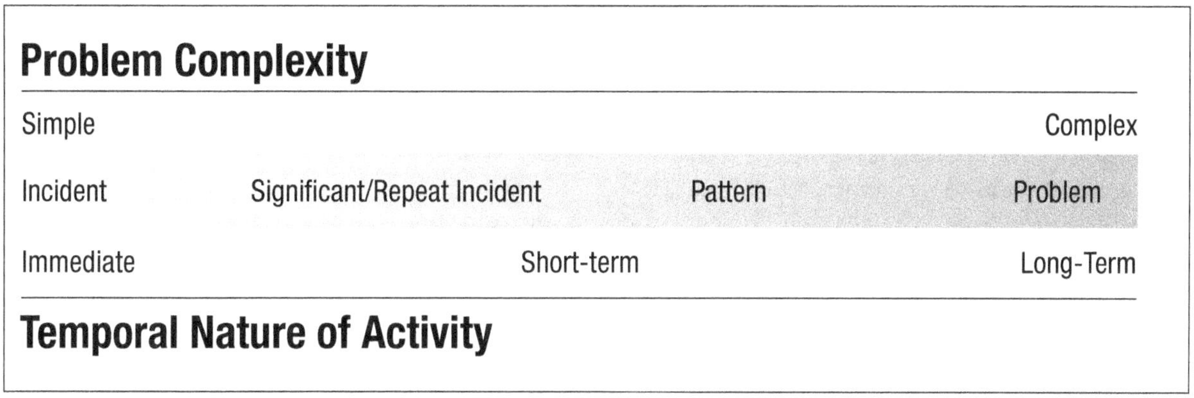

Problem Complexity

Simple			Complex
Incident	Significant/Repeat Incident	Pattern	Problem
Immediate		Short-term	Long-Term

Temporal Nature of Activity

Figure 2: Continuum of Problem Complexity

individual incidents to long-term compound problems—can be addressed successfully using this process. The components of the SARA process are:[12]

Scanning is the process of identifying problems of both small and large scope of concern to the public and the police, prioritizing those problems, and selecting problems for closer examination.

Analysis is the process of drawing conclusions about why the problem is occurring made based on official data, observation, and experience.

Response is the process, based on the analysis results, of identifying realistic responses appropriate to the scope of the problem and implementing them, which may require help from other agencies and the community.

Assessment is the process of determining if the response(s) to the problem worked, looking at implementation of the responses and the impact on the level of the problem.

Problem Complexity

In the Stratified Model, a system of crime reduction strategies is implemented for a range of short- and long-term problems. Notably, addressing short-term problems successfully helps to prevent long-term problems from surfacing or becoming significant issues. Long-term problems contain numerous patterns or repeat incidents (short-term problems) and by systematically identifying these short-term problems and responding to them effectively, long-term problems can be prevented.

The complexity of the problems is most easily understood in terms of the temporal nature of their development. That is, simpler problems, such as isolated incidents, are typically manifested over a very short period of time, where more complex problems, such as problem locations, develop over a longer period of time. Although a particular problem can sit anywhere on this continuum, in the Stratified Model, they are broken down into three temporal categories: 1) immediate problems: individual calls for service and crimes (incidents and serious incidents); 2) short-term problems: repeat incidents and patterns; and 3) long-term problems: problem locations, problem areas, problem offenders, problem victims, problem products, and compound problems. Figure 2 is an illustration of a continuum of complexity and temporal nature of problems addressed by police.

Immediate Problems

Problems considered "immediate" are isolated incidents that occur and are resolved within minutes, hours, or in some cases, days. They are responded to by patrol officers and detectives who utilize the investigative skills learned in basic police training and more intensive investigative training. Here, immediate activity is broken down into two categories:

Incidents are individual events which an officer typically responds to or discovers on while patrol. Incidents are citizen and officer generated calls for service and include crime, disorder, or service related tasks such as disturbances, robbery in progress, traffic accidents, subject stops, and traffic citations, all which usually occur and are resolved within minutes and/or hours—most of the time within one shift. Police officers typically conduct the preliminary investigation, and respond to incidents with the goal of resolving each incident as quickly and effectively as possible, while in accordance to the laws and policies of the jurisdiction and the police agency.

Serious incidents are individual events that arise from calls for service but are deemed more serious by laws and policies of the police department, thus require additional investigation and/or a more extensive immediate response. Serious incidents are events such as rapes, hostage negotiations, homicides, traffic fatalities, or armed robbery. They occur within minutes and/or hours but may take days, weeks, or in some cases, months to resolve. Typically, detectives or specially trained personnel (e.g., homicide detectives, traffic crash reconstructionists) conduct more comprehensive analysis and respond to these serious incidents with the goal of resolving the event according to the laws and policies of the jurisdiction and police agency, and in particular, to apprehend the offender(s).

Short-Term Problems

Problems considered "short-term" are those that occur over several days or weeks and typically require short-term versus immediate responses. Here, short-term problems are broken down into two categories—repeat incidents and patterns.[13]

Repeat incidents are two or more incidents that are similar in nature and have happened at the same place. These are related to common non-criminal disorder activity (e.g., disturbances, barking dogs, problem juveniles, or traffic crashes) or to interpersonal disputes and crimes between individuals who know one another (e.g., bar fights, domestic violence, drug offenses, and neighbor disputes). Repeat incidents happen within hours, days, and in some cases weeks of one another. Analysis of and response to repeat incidents focus on identifying addresses with repeat calls for service and resolving the immediate issue with a variety of responses from police, other agencies, and the community.

Patterns are two or more crimes that seem to be related by victim, offender, location, or property that typically occur

over days, weeks, or months. Patterns focus on crime in which the victim and the offender do not know one another (e.g., stranger rape, robbery, burglary, theft from/of vehicles, or grand theft). Analysis of patterns is systematically conducted by a crime analyst and responses focus on immediate, traditional crime reduction strategies employed by the police (e.g., directed patrol, field contacts, contacting victims and known offenders directly).

Long-Term Problems

Problems considered "long-term" are those that occur over several months, seasons, or years and stem from systematic opportunities created by everyday behavior and environment. Long-term problems require the most comprehensive analysis and response because a number of factors may contribute to the problem that has evolved over time, and responses will most likely require partnerships with the community and outside agencies. Problems can consist of common disorder activity (e.g., loud parties or speeding in residential neighborhoods) or serious criminal activity (e.g., armed robbery or residential burglary). The types of long-term activity include:

Problem locations are individual addresses (e.g., one convenience store) or types of places, also called risky facilities[14] (e.g., all convenience stores), at which there is a concentration of crime or problematic activity.

Problem areas, also called hot spots,[15] are relatively small areas (e.g., several block area) with a disproportionate amount of crime or disorder activity that is related.

Problem offenders, also called repeat offenders,[16] are either one person who has committed a disproportionate amount of crime or a group of offenders who share similar characteristics.

Problem victims, also called repeat victims, are either one person who has been victimized or a group of victims who share characteristics and have been targeted by different offenders (for more than 6 months).

Problem products, also called hot products, are classes of products being targeted that share characteristics that make them attractive and vulnerable in various situations to various types of offenders.

Compound problems are the highest level problems that encompass various locations, offenders, and victims and, in most cases, exist throughout an entire jurisdiction.

Accountability

The accountability element of the Stratified Model fundamentally ensures that the entire organization implements and maintains crime reduction efforts *consistently and effectively*. The accountability process centers on creating realistic expectations, systematically reviewing the progress of crime reduction activities, documenting the work being done, and evaluating the success of crime reduction efforts at each level. To accomplish this, the Stratified Model contains a meeting structure that corresponds to the stratification of the problem's complexity and the temporal nature of the activity addressed, as illustrated in Figure 3.

Each type of meeting is important because it serves a different purpose based on the type of activity addressed,

Daily meetings/briefings facilitate action-oriented accountability for strategies implemented for immediate and short-term problems. They are used to develop and monitor the implementation of strategies for significant incidents, repeat incidents, and patterns, as well as immediately assess the effectiveness of those strategies.

Weekly meetings facilitate action-oriented accountability within and/or among divisions (e.g., patrol, investigations, crime prevention, and media relations), so that employees can come together to develop, coordinate, and assess strategies implemented for short-term problems.

Monthly meetings facilitate evaluation-oriented accountability within geographic areas and support divisions, as well as across the entire agency. They are used to assess whether short-term crime reduction activities are effective, whether long-term problems are emerging, and to monitor the progress of ongoing long-term crime reduction strategies.

Meeting Frequency

Daily	Weekly	Monthly	Semi-Annually
Immediate		Short-Term	Long-Term

Temporal Nature of Activity

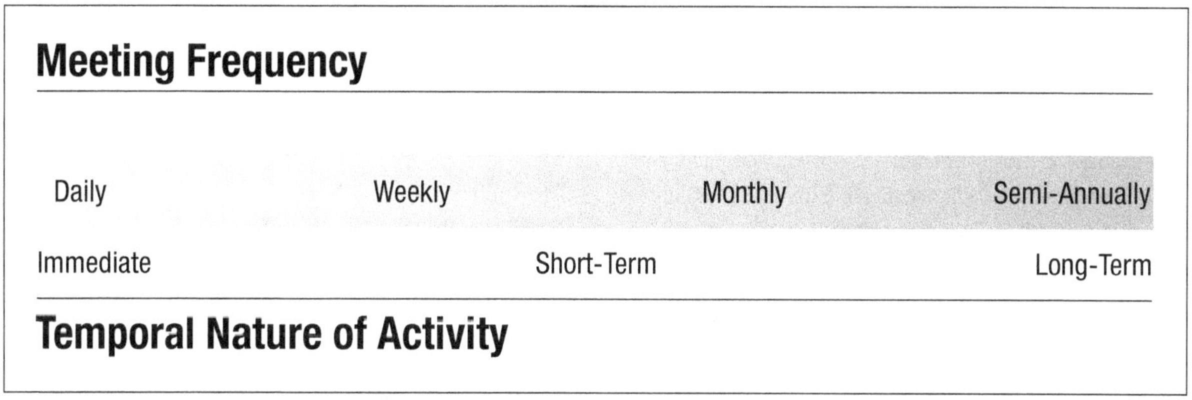

Figure 3: Continuum of Accountability Meeting Frequency

---

rank of personnel who attends, and how the meetings are documented. Daily and weekly meetings are *action oriented* because they are used to ensure that personnel are responding immediately, collaboratively, and appropriately. Monthly and semi-annual meetings are *evaluation oriented* because they are used to assess the overall effectiveness of short-term crime reduction and the progress and effectiveness of long-term crime reduction efforts. The following is a brief description of each type of meeting:

Semi-annual meetings facilitate evaluation-oriented accountability for the entire organization. They are used to examine long-term trends to determine the effectiveness of the agency's overall crime reduction approach and to identify new long-term problems to be addressed over the next six months or more, as well as to formulate agency goals and any new or modified strategies for the coming year(s).

Although the meeting structure is important to facilitate accountability, crime reduction efforts are part of the day-to-day operations of the police organization and are not done

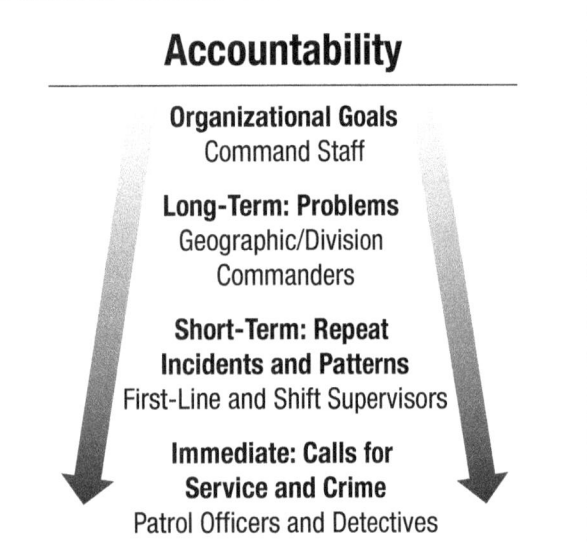

Accountability

Organizational Goals
Command Staff

Long-Term: Problems
Geographic/Division
Commanders

**Short-Term: Repeat
Incidents and Patterns**
First-Line and Shift Supervisors

**Immediate: Calls for
Service and Crime**
Patrol Officers and Detectives

*Figure 4: Hierarchy of Crime Reduction Responsibility
and Accountability*

only in preparation for a meeting. As noted earlier, people in the organization are responsible for crime reduction at a level appropriate to their rank and responsibilities, and all but line-level officers are responsible for holding a lower rank accountable for their efforts. Ultimately, the agency's top leaders hold all people accountable for the overall outcomes. Figure 4 is an illustration of the hierarchy of crime reduction responsibility and accountability.

Developing Goals and Objectives for Crime Reduction

In order to prioritize crime reduction efforts and provide focus for the problem solving process, an agency first develops explicit goals and objectives that are used to guide the agency and to provide specific measures by which to assess the agency's success in reducing crime and disorder. These goals are different than goals and objectives traditionally formulated in police organizations for a 3 to 5 year *strategic plan*. Instead, they refer to specific goals relating to strategies implemented in the context of the Stratified Model to reduce crime. In addition, these goals are intentionally general since their main purposes are to

help prioritize crime reduction efforts at each level of the Stratified Model and to set targets that the agency seeks to achieve for crime reduction.

To make a crime reduction goal actionable and relevant in the day-to-day operations of the agency, not only is the outcome of the goal specified, but so are the success indicators, baseline and target measurements, strategies, and measurements of performance. Importantly, the outcomes, methods, and outputs are differentiated in order to assess both the process (i.e., whether strategies were implemented effectively) and impact (i.e., whether the strategies decreased crime) of the crime reduction strategies. The following are descriptions of each component of crime reduction goals. Table 1 (on page 13) provides an example of one goal and its components.

Crime reduction goal: This is the desired outcome and is generally stated. It denotes a specific type of activity (e.g., violent crime, burglary, disorder, fear of crime) as well as the geographic area (e.g., citywide, countywide, District 1). Most likely, large jurisdictions will develop goals for geographic regions separately.

Success indicator: This component specifies the type of activity that is used to measure the impact of the crime reduction strategies (i.e., outcome). The purpose of this component is to denote a specific measurement relevant to the crime reduction goal, because using general measurements such as Uniform Crime Report (UCR) Part I Crime categories can mask changes in the *specific* crimes that are being addressed. For example, instead of using all UCR Part I violent crime (homicide, rape, robbery, and aggravated assault) to measure a goal to reduce violent crime, the success indicator measures specific types of violent crime that the agency has identified as a problem—in their jurisdiction—such as non-domestic aggravated assault and street robbery. Similarly, instead of using data for all burglaries to measure a goal, the success indicator can measure residential or commercial burglary separately, or, even more specifically, it can measure residential burglary at single family homes (not apartments).

The success indicator also specifies the level of desired success. This is normally depicted as a percent decrease in the type of activity (e.g., 10 percent decrease). The percent to

Table 1: Crime Reduction Goal Example

Component	Description
Goal	Reduce violent crime citywide
Success Indicators	Reduce non-domestic aggravated assault and street robbery by 10 percent Priority: Districts 1 and 2 (account for 70 percent of these crimes)
Baseline	Non-domestic aggravated assaults=550; Districts 1 and 2=385 Street robbery=450; Districts 1 and 2=315 Baseline time period: Jan-08 to Dec-10 (average of three years)
Target	Non-domestic aggravated assault=495; Districts 1 and 2=347 Street robberies=405; Districts 1 and 2=284 Target time period: Jan-11 to Dec-11
Strategies	Improve data collection in police reports (immediate) Address patterns (short-term) Address problem locations and offenders (long-term)
Performance Indicators	Improvement in police report quality Number of arrests and case clearances Number of patterns identified and resolved successfully Number of problem offenders and locations identified and addressed successfully Cost analysis of responses deployed

use is relative to the goal and the jurisdiction and is based on previous crime levels, the level of resources available to the agency, and a qualitative decision by the agency's leaders based on their knowledge and experience about what is a realistic goal for their agency.

Lastly, in some cases geographic area is specified within the success indicator. This is different than specifying the geographic area in the goal statement, in that a geographic area listed here indicates that even though the overall goal may apply to the entire jurisdiction, the responses will be prioritized in the listed area.

Baseline: This is the initial measurement of success indicator. The value is listed as well as the time period under consideration and the method of computation. The measurement can reflect frequency or counts of a year of data or it can reflect a rate or an average over several years, depending on the data available and the nature of the activity.

Target: This is the desired level of success and is computed based on the percent indicated in the success indicator and the baseline measurement. It is typically computed for 1 year, which is the evaluation period of the goal.

Strategies: The strategies listed here for each goal address crime reduction efforts that the agency will implement *simultaneously* at each level of the organization, and are selected based on the particular type of crime or disorder problem outlined in the goal (e.g., repeat incidents are used for reducing disorder short-term; patterns for street robbery; problem locations for assaults at bars).

Performance indicators: These are a list of the process outcomes of crime reduction activities (i.e., outputs). Examples include officer activity, such as number of arrests and cleared cases; rate of success in addressing specific types of short-term and long-term activity, such as percent of patterns and problem locations that were responded to successfully; and an analysis of the additional operational costs of the responses, such as overtime and equipment purchases.

Immediate Crime Reduction

The crime reduction strategies employed at the immediate level for incidents are already solidly institutionalized into most police organizations. The skills and knowledge needed to answer calls for service effectively and investigate crimes is covered by a wide range of established introductory and specialized training offered through police academies and in-service training. Accountability for officers and detectives is already built into a police department's organizational policies and systems, so these processes are not discussed in this guidebook. However, for the Stratified Model to be effectively implemented into an agency, improvements and enhancements in data collection will be necessary. In addition, systematic accountability of the most serious incidents can be improved. These two issues are discussed in this section.

Data Collection from Incidents

Although crime reduction strategies for addressing immediate activity are already institutionalized into policing, implementing the Stratified Model requires improvement in the data collection process for incidents. Analyses of the more complex types of problems are based on the data collected at the incident level (e.g., calls for service, field information cards, crime reports, and arrests). Dispatchers, officers, and detectives—as part of their normal duties—are data collectors, with sergeants and other supervisors playing an important role in overseeing the quality of these data.

Police reports are typically written for prosecution purposes (i.e., information to establish the crime and probable cause) and often do not include specific information that is useful and imperative for effective analysis of more complex problems. Thus, implementing the Stratified Model requires police to capture additional information concerning specific methods of the crime, the routine activities of the individuals, and the environment of the place. Information collected is not only used to resolve an individual incident, but is also used to identify and understand larger, more complex problems. Both the quantitative data of a police report (i.e., standardized fields such as date, time, and location) and the qualitative data (i.e., the police narrative) should be improved so that the information also informs analysis at higher levels in the model. Information about modus operandi, crime prevention methods used, and the surrounding environment is not typically or consistently

collected in many police report narratives, but it must be for effective use in analysis for crime reduction strategies.[19]

Correspondingly, investigative interviews with suspects typically focus on establishing guilt, and detectives do not consistently ask questions that yield information that is helpful beyond a particular case. In addition to asking suspects traditional questions that determine guilt based on elements of crime, detectives should also ask questions that determine *why* the person committed the crime in that circumstance at that time to determine opportunities and the offenders' perceptions of risk. For example: "Why did you select this house to burglarize? Why did you choose that person in that circumstance to rob?" The information gathered, though not terribly relevant for that particular investigation for prosecution purposes, can be analyzed along with other interviews and can contribute to the understanding of why the patterns and problems are occurring in the local context.

Field information/interview data are other examples of data that should be improved. Field information/interview cards taken by patrol officers of suspicious persons, vehicles, and situations are an important source of intelligence that can be used in pattern and problem analysis. However, many agencies simply document date, time, person information, and a short narrative of the incident. Categories that denote the behavior of the person at the time of contact (e.g., sitting, riding a bike, walking, sleeping) and the nature of the environment (e.g., alley, sidewalk, parking lot, vacant building) assist in sorting and grouping the field information for analysis. This additional information can be collected easily through simple check boxes on paper cards or fields with drop down menus in electronic forms.

There are many other ways in which police data can and need to be improved to assist in the implementation of effective crime reduction strategies (e.g., data related to geography, offenders, victims, property). Such improvements can be facilitated by computer systems that are often distinct to specific jurisdictions, so they must be considered on an individual agency basis. Importantly, improving data quality is an integral part in successfully using crime analysis within the problem solving process. However, in order for any of these data collection improvements to impact the implementation of strategies within the Stratified Model, they must be enacted consistently and throughout the entire organization. It is not enough to have officers on one shift or in a specialized unit follow these enhanced data collection procedures. All police reports must be improved in order for the data to be reliable and analysis useful. Prioritization of data collection and accountability are the key to consistency of data collection.

Prioritization refers to determining which types and characteristics of crime are important and necessary. It may not be necessary or realistic to improve the data collection of all police reports, so the enhanced data collection procedures should be guided by the agency's goals for crime reduction. For example, an agency addressing robberies and burglaries would focus on data collection improvements for these two crimes, both in the technology (i.e., report writing software and records management system requirements) and in report writing by personnel (i.e., content of report narratives).

Accountability for improved data collection lies squarely on the shoulders of the first-line supervisors in the agency—in patrol, criminal investigations, and specialized units. In most police departments, sergeants review and approve police reports, thus they determine the quality of police reports. Just as reports should be written consistently, approval of their quality should be done consistently as well. It is common in many agencies that particular sergeants are less stringent in their approval of reports. Because of this, first-line supervisors also need to be held accountable by their supervisors for the quality of the reports they approve to ensure all data are being collected consistently.

Lastly, police leaders should prioritize obtaining systems for effective data collection as well as enforce policies that ensure the human factor of data collection is also effective. If the Stratified Model is to be implemented successfully, data collection and its quality must be a high priority, even if funding for technology is not available or not considered necessary (e.g., in a small agency).

Significant Incidents

Significant incidents are specific serious incidents that are proactively identified by an agency as the highest priority because of their relationship to the agency's crime reduc-

tion goals, seriousness, and/or their political and social nature (e.g., mass shooting, assault of the city's mayor, a violent robbery, officer involved shooting). Although strategies for addressing all serious incidents are currently institutionalized through the criminal investigations process, prioritizing particular incidents for systematic accountability at a higher level in the organization (e.g., command level) can improve both the effectiveness and the consistency of these strategies. Thus, the process outlined in this section provides a system for identifying and enhancing the accountability for these incidents.

Significant Incident Identification

The process of identifying the significant incidents is unique to each agency and requires the leadership of the agency to develop criteria for their selection based on the agency's goals, as well as other social and political concerns within that jurisdiction. Although it may be obvious when significant incidents such as a school shooting occur, the criteria would vary by the size of the agency as well as the amount and seriousness of crime occurring in a particular jurisdiction. For example, in a small agency with low levels of crime, a significant incident may be any robbery or burglary involving the loss of $10,000 or more worth of property, whereas in a large agency these types of incidents would not be considered significant because they happen more often.

A more specific example comes from the Port St. Lucie, Florida Police Department, which serves a population of 160,000 and has a crime rate lower than the national average. That agency uses the following criteria to select significant incidents: all suspicious deaths, all shootings, home invasion robberies, serious violent gang crime, officer safety incidents, as well as armed robbery, violent sex crimes, abductions, and serious aggravated battery committed by strangers, and property crimes involving city property, city officials, and officer safety incidents. Consequently, the criteria should be developed for an agency so that a manageable number of significant incidents are identified on a daily basis, to make sure that the additional accountability procedures carried out for these incidents are realistic within the confines of the other crime reduction work being conducted in the agency.

Table 2: Significant Incident Report Example

SIGNIFICANT INCIDENTS: March 10, 2011

Persons Crime

Case #	Offense	Date/Time	Location	Synopsis
2011-005409	Shooting	3/6/2011: 2330	1334 SW Baylor Blvd (Parking Lot of Lucky's Lounge)	A group of black male subjects had a confrontation in the parking lot. One suspect pulled out a handgun and fired several shots at the victim who was sitting in a vehicle. Approximately 4 to 5 suspects fled in a gold Impala. The victim's vehicle had small bullet fragments on the inside of the passenger door and thirteen 9mm casings were found in the area.

Property Crime

Case #	Offense	Date/Time	Location	Synopsis
2011-0005674	Burglary	3/10/2011: 0300 to 0400	City Public Works Yard	Vandalism of buildings and equipment inside. Over $50,000 worth of damage with some gang graffiti painted on walls inside buildings.
2011-0005665	Theft from Auto	3/9/2011: 2000 to 2300	1456 E Symbolica Circle	Theft from city mayor's personal vehicle of city issued laptop and paperwork along with other smaller personal items left in vehicle.

Once the criteria are developed, incidents are reviewed every day and those that meet the criteria are briefly summarized and presented in a report for command staff to review and/or to discuss in a daily briefing. Table 2 is an example of an analysis product that supports the identification of significant incidents.

Significant Incident Analysis and Response

Analysis and response of all incidents are initiated by patrol or criminal investigations immediately; however, significant incidents selected through this process are those that require additional resources, collaboration, and/or sensitive media releases. These incidents most likely involve the criminal investigations division of the agency (versus patrol). However, specific techniques of analysis and response (i.e., investigation) are not discussed here because they are already institutionalized into most police agencies' operations.

Significant Incident Accountability and Assessment

As with every level in the Stratified Model, accountability processes for significant incidents include systematically reviewing progress of implemented strategies, documenting the work being done, and evaluating the success of the strategies. Although detectives are primarily responsible for the day-to-day investigations of significant incidents, because they are the most serious incidents and have been prioritized by the agency, as part of the Stratified Model, the strategies are also consistently monitored by the criminal investigations commander and the agency's command level.

Accountability for significant incident investigations is facilitated by the command staff of the agency in which they hold the criminal investigation division commander accountable. More specific and informal status updates of the investigations occur within the criminal investigation division among the detectives, supervisors, and managers, but weekly and monthly updates would also occur to track the overall investigative strategies and their effectiveness. Although specific case files are kept by detectives, to track the ongoing progress of investigations, weekly documentation would be kept by the criminal investigations manager to ensure that more general information is being documented for accountability purposes (versus prosecutor purposes) in order to brief the criminal investigations commander. The following is an example of how one significant incident would be tracked:

Significant incident summary (residential robbery):
Two white male suspects knocked on the 66-year-old victim's front door while he was in the backyard of his residence. When he answered the door, one suspect demanded money while shoving a small black semi-automatic pistol in the victim's ribs. The other suspect punched the victim in the face knocking him to the ground and stole his wallet containing $150 and credit cards.

Analysis: The K-9 unit responded and tracked the suspects to a vacant lot nearby where witnesses reported seeing the suspects enter a vehicle parked on the other side. Witnesses provided additional information about the suspects' descriptions: 1) White male, 20-30 years of age, 5'11" – 6'1", 160-180 lbs, brown shoulder length hair, and 2) White male, dark complexion, 20-30 years of age, 5'8" – 5'9", 150-170 lbs, short hair. Suspects were seen leaving in a small metallic green two door vehicle, possibly a Toyota or Mitsubishi. The victim had just cashed two checks at a check cashing store in the neighborhood prior to the incident.

Investigative responses implemented: Additional interviews with victim and witnesses. Detective was able to retrieve store video of a white male using the victim's credit card in a nearby retail store.

Action items for next meeting: Distribute suspect bulletin. Contact crime stoppers. Determine if video image is good enough to be entered into the facial recognition database.

Results (assessment): Ongoing.

The documentation would then be used for several purposes. The criminal investigations manager would use the summaries to track responses and follow up on action items from previous weeks. The criminal investigations commander would use them to hold the criminal investigations

manager accountable as well as report on the progress of the investigation to the agency's command staff where a general overview (versus specific details) of the investigations and their results are most important. Notably, toward the end of the guide, the section on organizational accountability lays out, in more detail, how the Stratified Model's meeting structure facilitates the accountability and evaluation of crime reduction strategies implemented for significant incidents as well as the other levels.

Short-Term Crime Reduction

Many police departments focus on short-term crime reduction, but do not employ the problem solving process consistently or use crime analysis in a systematic way. The Stratified Model provides structure and guidance for short-term crime reduction through consistent and routine identification and analysis of short-term problems, an organized approach to implementing responses, and a system accountability and documentation for evaluation. Importantly, many police agencies focus primarily on crime, while the Stratified Model presents strategies for both crime and disorder.

Repeat Incidents

Repeat incidents are disorder, quality of life, and interpersonal crime issues that are recurring at the same locations/areas.[20] More specifically, quality of life issues are common, non-criminal disorder activity, such as disturbances, barking dogs, problem juveniles, or traffic crashes, and interpersonal crimes are disputes and criminal incidents between individuals who know one another, such as bar fights, domestic violence, and neighbor disputes. The goal of addressing repeat incidents is to resolve them immediately before they manifest into larger, long-term problems.

Repeat Incident Identification

Calls for service data are the key data source used to identify repeat incidents because they are available immediately and contain both criminal and non-criminal activity. The call data are used to identify individual locations that have had multiple calls for service over several weeks.

Table 3: Repeat Incident Report Example

District 1: January 4 – 31, 2011
1232 W BAYSHORE RD

DESCRIPTION	DATE/TIME	DAY	DISPOSITION	INCIDENT#	OFFICER ID#
NEIGHBOR TROUBLE	1/24/2011 18:20	MON	FI CARD	90125001063	265
NOISE COMPLAINT	1/19/2011 23:21	WED	GOA	90120001736	346
NOISE COMPLAINT	1/19/2011 22:47	WED	REPORT	90120001700	245
NOISE COMPLAINT	1/18/2011 22:36	TUE	FI CARD	90119001485	510
NEIGHBOR TROUBLE	1/13/2011 15:49	THU	RESOLVED	90114000962	245

Because calls for service provide only a limited amount of detail about the nature of the activity that is occurring, the analysis strategy for repeat incidents is to use the data to identify potential repeat incident locations through a report and then follow up with a more in depth examination of the underlying activity at the location to determine if the activity indicated by the calls is related.

To focus repeat incident identification, particular types of calls for service that indicate similar activity are combined to produce one or more repeat incident reports. For example, a disorder-related repeat incident report includes an analysis of calls such as disturbances, loud noise, and suspicious activity, fights, and narcotics calls. However, reports focusing on other types of activity, such as false alarms, traffic accidents, animal calls, code violations, and domestic violence, require the examination of a different combination of call types. The number of reports and types of calls selected depends on the nature of the activity, the call codes, as well as the agency's goals and resources.

To prioritize crime reduction efforts and to create realistic expectations for personnel, a standardized report is produced weekly for the previous 28 days (i.e., 28 days from whenever the report is produced) that sets a threshold for the number of calls. That is, only those locations that have had, for example, three or more calls in a 28 day period, will appear on the report. Sworn personnel and crime analysts work together to determine the type of calls and threshold number of calls that are appropriate for a particular report. The results of the report should be a realistic number of addresses that can be addressed by the appropriate staff each week.

The information included on each report is fairly restricted because of the limited nature of calls for service data. It includes the date, day, and time of the call, type of call, disposition of the call, case number, and officer that responded. This information assists personnel in determining whether the activity is related superficially or whether the repeat incidents at a location should be further investigated (i.e., analyzed). Table 3 is an example of one address within a repeat incident report that is focused on disorder activity:

Repeat Incident Analysis and Response

In most cases, the analysis of a repeat incident location—that is, understanding the underlying cause of the recurring calls at a location—requires additional data collection (e.g., observation and interviews) to determine the cause of the problem, so a tailored response can be implemented. As shown in Table 3, 1232 W Bayshore Rd (a single-family residence) has had five calls for service—two calls for neighbor trouble and three for noise complaints over 9 days. Although the calls all occur in the late afternoon and evening hours, it is difficult to determine the underlying reason for these calls from this report, which is why it would be necessary to talk to the responding officers and potentially the residents themselves. Only after additional information has been gathered and it's been determined the activity is related can a tailored response be developed. In some cases, the additional analysis may indicate the calls are not related, so no response is necessary.

In a typical police organization, the Stratified Model assigns the first-line patrol supervisors the responsibility for conducting problem solving of repeat incident locations;

however, this may vary by organization size and rank structure. In addition, responsibility for repeat incident locations would also be assigned according to geographic region. Thus, first-line supervisors are responsible for doing the following for repeat incident locations in their geographic areas:

■ Reviewing the repeat incident report each week and selecting locations for analysis

■ Overseeing analysis of locations to determine if calls are related

■ Selecting locations for response as well as determining what response(s) are appropriate

■ Overseeing the implementation of responses

■ Tracking responses

■ Determining if and when the repeat incident is resolved

Patrol officers would assist their supervisors in the analysis of and response to repeat incident locations. Repeat incident responses focus on developing more permanent solutions than what was previously done for the individual calls and would likely engage other entities as appropriate—for example, other divisions within the agency (e.g., traffic unit, animal control, domestic violence unit), county social services, code enforcement, neighborhood associations, business owners, etc. The purpose of addressing repeat incident locations is to resolve the short-term recurring issues as quickly and effectively as possible so that they don't expend the organization's resources with additional calls and don't become larger, long-term problems.[21]

Repeat Incident Accountability and Assessment

The accountability processes for repeat incidents include systematically reviewing the progress of responses, documenting the work being done, and evaluating the success of the responses. If first-line supervisors are responsible for addressing repeat incident locations, their supervisors (typically responsible for the same geographic area or shift) hold them accountable for implementing appropriate responses and whether the responses worked (e.g., did calls for service reduce or stop at that location?).

Ideally, weekly meetings (or other systematic communication methods) are used to hold first-line supervisors accountable for responding to newly identified repeat incident locations, continuing responses to previously identified locations, and evaluating whether implemented responses are working. Weekly documentation of each repeat incident location includes a short, succinct summary of the nature of the activity, the responses implemented, and the results. The primary purpose of the documentation is to keep track of the progress of the problem-solving process for each location to ensure planned responses are actually implemented, as well as to determine when and if the response was successful. The following is an example of how the documentation taken for one repeat incident (in Table 3 on page 18) might be formatted:

Scan: Over the last 9 days, five calls occurring during the week in the late afternoon/evening hours related to noise complaints and neighbor trouble were reported at 1232 W Bayshore Rd. Two calls resulted in FI cards, one was resolved, and another resulted in a report.

Analysis: Interviews with responding officers and residents indicate that these calls are all related to activity in which the teenage children are playing loud music while hanging out in the garage. The police report was the result of a fight between two intoxicated teens in the garage.

Response: Officer Jones responded to the address to speak with the parents who were uncooperative. The officer has contacted the owner of the home (residents are renters) who has warned the residents about the noise and potential illegal activity (underage drinking).

Assessment: No further calls were documented in the month of February. Repeat incident resolved.

Toward the end of the guide, the section on organizational accountability lays out, in more detail, how the Stratified Model's meeting structure facilitates the accountability and evaluation of crime reduction strategies implemented for repeat incidents as well as for the other levels.

Patterns

Patterns are two or more crimes that seem to be related by victim, offender, location, or property that typically occur over days, weeks, or months.[22] They are *not* a list of cases or simple counts of crimes in a set time period. Patterns focus on crime in which the victim and the offender do not know one another, such as robbery, burglary, and theft from vehicle. The goal of crime reduction strategies implemented for short-term patterns is to apprehend offenders, clear cases, and prevent similar crimes from happening before they become larger, long-term problems.

Pattern Identification and Analysis

Most importantly, systematic identification and analysis of patterns require dedicated crime analysis personnel trained in pattern identification methodology and local databases. Crime analysts use initial crime report data to identify patterns because these data provide the most accurate and timely information for crime. Calls for service should not be used for pattern analysis, because specific information on method of the crime, suspect information, and vehicle information is required for effective pattern analysis and should be automated for efficient and effective analysis. Even though this guidebook does not cover the extensive process of identifying patterns,[23] it is important to distinguish the different types of patterns that can be identified and that warrant a response. They include:[24]

Series: A group of similar crimes thought to be committed by the same individual or group of individuals acting in concert. Example: Four commercial arsons citywide in which a black male, between the ages of 45–50, wearing yellow sweatpants, a black hooded sweatshirt, and a yellow "Yankees" cap, was observed leaving the commercial structures immediately after the fire alarm was triggered.

Spree: A specific type of series characterized by high frequency of criminal activity within a remarkably short time frame, to the extent that the activity appears almost continuous. Example: A rash of thefts from auto at a parking garage over the course of 1 hour.

Hot Prey: A group of crimes committed by one or more individuals, involving victims who share similar physical characteristics and/or engage in similar behavior. Example: Five home invasion robberies of Asian immigrant families occurring throughout the city over 6 weeks.

Hot Product: A group of crimes committed by one or more individuals in which a unique type of property is targeted for theft. Example: Sixteen thefts of GPS units from vehicles at residential and commercial places in 3 weeks.

Hot Spot: A group of similar crimes committed by one or more individuals at locations within close proximity to one another. Example: Eight daytime burglaries over the past 4 weeks at a suburban residential subdivision, with no notable similarities in method of entry or known suspects.

Hot Place: A group of similar crimes committed by one or more individuals at the same location. Example: A local movie theatre that has experienced 15 thefts from auto, several incidents of graffiti on the building, and two strong-arm robberies in the parking lot over the course of 1 month.

Hot Setting: A group of similar crimes committed by one or more individuals that are primarily related by type of place where crimes occurred. Example: Eleven late night robberies of 24-hour convenience stores throughout the city by different offenders over 2 weeks.

Once a pattern is identified, a standardized crime pattern bulletin is created that is short, succinct, and provides a summary of crimes within the pattern. In general, information that is provided in a crime pattern bulletin focuses on how the crimes were committed (i.e., modus operandi), who potentially committed them (i.e., suspects seen by witnesses, persons who were field interviewed in the area, or known offenders living in the area), when they occurred, and where they occurred. The goal in describing these aspects of a pattern is to summarize all the information from the cases together, not to restate each case. Each bulletin contains components that when combined provide a complete picture of the pattern.[25] Most crime analysts make every effort to make their pattern bulletins one page for ease of reading and to help keep the information succinct. Figure 5 on page 21 is an example of a model crime pattern bulletin.

Pattern Reponses

The Stratified Model indicates that, in a typical agency, sergeants or lieutenants (depending on the size of the organization) in patrol are assigned responsibility of addressing patterns according to when and where they occur. A general

 **Police Department**
Crime Analysis Unit

Bulletin #: 2010-246
Released: November 3, 2010

FOR LAW ENFORCEMENT USE ONLY

Hotspot: Residential Burglaries in Beat 31

Number of Incidents:	7
Date Range:	October 22, 2010 – November 3, 2010
Time Range:	All incidents occurred during the day (between 0900 and 1620) during the week
Target:	Single family homes
Property Taken:	TVs, computers, cash jewelry
General Location:	North of Becker Rd and East of Darwin Rd; Beat 31
MO:	Forced entry in all incidents, either front or rear slider/cabana door

 Known Burglary Offenders:

 John Smith
210 S. Mablen St.
W/M, DOB: 01/15/90, 20 yrs

 Mike Jones
420 E. Midland Rd.
W/M, DOB: 05/16/92, 18 yrs

 Jake Evans
519 E. Rail Av.
B/M, DOB 09/01/84, 26 yrs

Map #	Case #	Date	Time	Day	Address	Entry	Property Taken
1	09-10591	10/22/10	1000-1215	Fri	4600 S Tacture Ter	Front door-forced	N/A Ransacked
2	09-10593	10/22/10	1000-1530	Fri	4401 S Lander Ln	Front door-forced	TV, Jewelry
3	09-10798	10/28/10	0945-1245	Thu	451 W Treebird Dr	Rear screen cut	Jewelry, Cash
4	09-10825	10/28/10	1340-1620	Thu	337 W Gale Dr	Rear slider-pry	TV, Computer
5	09-10829	10/29/10	0930-1500	Fri	200 S Ridgecrest Dr	Cabana door-pry	N/A
6	09-10874	11/02/10	0900-1400	Tue	4815 W Boxing Ci	Rear slider-pry	Cash
7	09-10875	11/02/10	1000-1200	Tue	109 W Chadwick Ct	Front door-forced	N/A Ransacked

All data presented in this bulletin (e.g., incidents, names, and addresses) are sample data and do not represent actual crime, people, or places.

Figure 5: Crime Pattern Bulletin Example

rule to help determine which rank should be responsible for patterns in a specific agency is to look to the highest rank working the midnight shift in patrol. For example, in an agency where patrol lieutenants are the highest rank working midnights, all patrol lieutenants (day, evening, and midnights) would be assigned responsibility. To allocate a realistic workload and ensure in depth knowledge of resources available for response, the lieutenant working *when and where* each pattern is occurring would be assigned the responsibility of ensuring and coordinating the agency's *immediate* response.

Patterns require immediate responses primarily at the time when the crimes in the pattern are occurring, which is why the Stratified Model dictates that patrol takes the lead since it is active 24 hours a day, 7 days a week.[26] Other divisions within the agency, such as criminal investigations, special operations, and crime prevention assist with responses that are implemented during waking hours as their functions and capabilities dictate. Research and practice has shown that effective and appropriate responses to short-term patterns consist primarily of strategies that police departments currently use.[27] Thus, responses are broken down into those that must be implemented when and where the pattern is occurring (implemented by patrol) and others that are implemented during waking and/or business hours (typically implemented by support divisions).[28]

Responses Implemented When and Where the Pattern is Occurring

Directed patrol: Patrol in the areas and times in which a pattern is occurring in cars, on bikes, or on foot. The objective is to find offenders committing a crime or to deter offenders by increasing their perceived risk of being caught.

Field contacts: While conducting directed patrol, people are stopped and contacted in the pattern area. The objective is to deter offenders from committing crime by increasing their perceived risk as well as provide potential investigative leads for patterns analysis and criminal investigations.[29]

Surveillance: This response requires waiting in a particular area at a particular time for a crime to happen in order to make an arrest. This is often used in the most specific patterns because personnel costs are very high (e.g., officer

overtime). In the pattern bulletin, the analyst provides the best time and place for surveillance to take place.[30]

"Sting" or "bait" operations: This response requires a situation where people or property that have been targeted in a particular pattern are put out as "bait" for offenders (e.g., theft from vehicles). The objective is to arrest the offender in the act or record offenders committing the crimes when the bait is taken. In the pattern bulletin, the analyst provides the best time and place for the bait operation to take place.[31]

Responses Implemented During Waking and/or Business Hours

Clearing cases/assigning a pattern to a detective: This is the process of detectives using one or two solved cases in the pattern to investigate and solve the other cases in the pattern through witness identification, evidence, or confession. To facilitate this process, a pattern is assigned to one detective who then investigates the assigned crimes within the pattern simultaneously.

Contacting known offenders: Crime pattern theory[32] tells us that offenders tend to commit crimes in areas they are familiar with, which is often near where they work or live. In most bulletins, investigative leads obtained from field information (i.e., FI cards) and known offenders living in the area are provided to supply individuals as leads that can be contacted.

Contacting potential victims directly: Research shows that crime prevention education works best when it is targeted at specific victims, times, and areas.[33] This response includes contacting specific groups of citizens, residents, or businesses that are most relevant to a particular pattern. The contact can be made in person, through a letter via postal mail, through flyers left at homes or businesses, or through an electronic phone system (i.e., reverse 911). The information includes details of the pattern, crime prevention advice, and contact information for the police. Crime prevention advice includes suggestions with immediate results (e.g., lock doors and windows) and those with more long-term results (e.g., installing video surveillance equipment or alarms).[34]

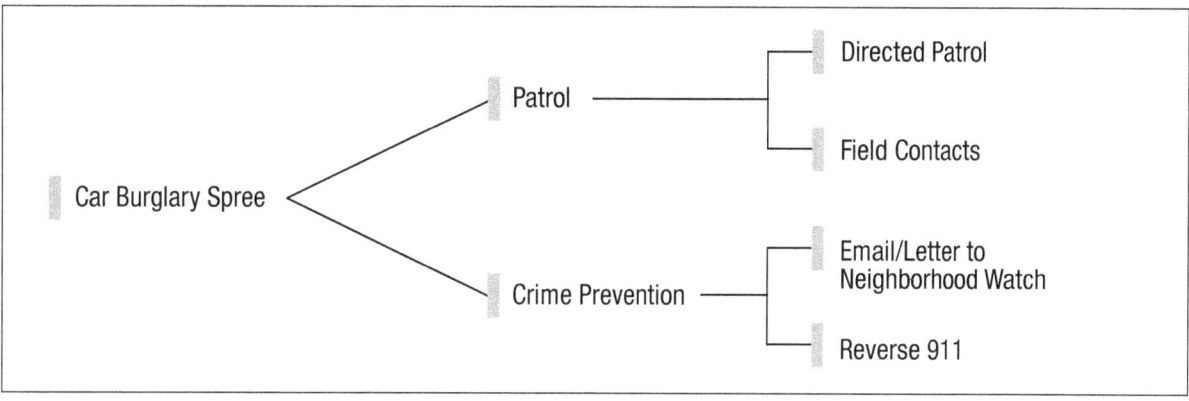

Figure 6: Responses to a Car Burglary Spree

Providing pattern information to the public: By disseminating synthesized and sanitized (i.e., condensed and sensitive information removed) patterns to the general public, people are encouraged to provide additional information ("tips") on known crimes, as well as to report crimes that have not yet been reported. Also, offenders might be deterred from continuing their offending. Information about patterns also provides specific crime prevention advice to a general audience, and encourages individuals to protect themselves. Media such as newspapers, radio, television, and the Internet are used to provide this information.[35]

From these strategies, a checklist of responses can be developed to provide a simple way for managers to select appropriate responses for each pattern. The checklist would be tailored based on the organizational structure of the police agency implementing the Stratified Model and the functions of each division/unit. Note that there are some duplicate categories since multiple divisions could respond similarly.

Patrol

☐ Directed marked patrol in the pattern area (car, bike, foot)

☐ Unmarked patrol in the pattern area (car, foot)

☐ Specialized unit (stops people in pattern area, conduct surveillance, etc.)

Criminal investigations

☐ Crimes in pattern assigned to one detective

☐ Contact known offenders (provided by analysis)

☐ Bait car/property/victim placed in the pattern area

☐ Unmarked patrol/surveillance in the pattern area (car, foot)

☐ Specialized unit (stops people in pattern area, conduct surveillance, etc.)

Crime prevention and public information

☐ Contact potential victims directly (letters, flyers, in person, reverse 911)

☐ Post sanitized patterns on police department web page

☐ Publish media alert

Within the Stratified Model, it is the responsibility of the patrol supervisor assigned to the individual pattern to select and coordinate the appropriate responses. The combination and intensity of responses depends on the nature of the specific pattern.[36] For example, a spree of car burglaries in an apartment complex one afternoon requires less response than a street robbery series occurring in a large primarily residential area. Figure 6 above and Figure 7 on page 24 illustrate the different set of responses that might be implemented for these two distinct patterns. Thus, consideration of the seriousness of a pattern, the other activity occurring in the jurisdiction, and the current workload of the agency, as well as the resources available—all are used to determine the exact responses implemented for a specific pattern.

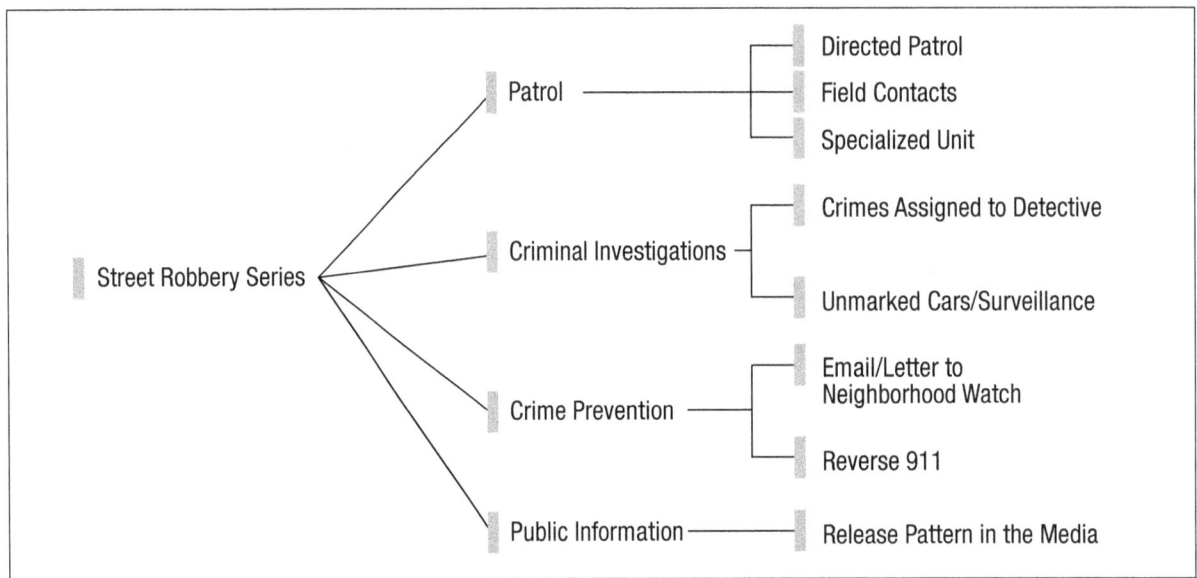

Figure 7: Responses to a Street Robbery Series

An important part of a system of response and accountability is documenting the work that is done for each pattern. This information is used to develop performance measures as well as hold personnel accountable for implementing responses quickly and effectively. Pattern responses can be documented a number of ways; some examples include:

Report: A paper or electronic form can also be used for the person responsible for the pattern (i.e., shift lieutenant) to log officers' and detectives' activity for each pattern. It includes the pattern number as well as fields for logging date, time, location, and activity generated. These forms summarize a wide variety of activity communicated to the supervisor for each pattern separately.

Computer-aided dispatch and/or case management system: When officers and detectives implement responses in a pattern area, they can record the information through the dispatch system and their case management system, respectively. If a common reference code is used, such as the pattern number, this information can be accessed at a later date and summarized (in a report) to document the range of responses for a pattern.

Intranet site: In agencies where officers have access to a police department intranet site through laptops in their cars, responses can be documented online. For example, in the Port St. Lucie, Florida Police Department when a pattern is identified by the crime analysts, the pattern bulletins are immediately posted to the agency's intranet system for review by sworn personnel. A pattern discussion board (i.e., "thread") provides officers the capability to post information about their responses as well as their knowledge of the pattern area, known offenders, or of field interviews that have been conducted. It also allows supervisors to monitor if appropriate responses are taking place. The entries occur in "real time," which allows information that was once passed by word of mouth to be seen by all personnel. This helps to inform all police personnel who are responsible for responding to a pattern about the progress of the current pattern response. Again, this information can be accessed in real time or at a later date and summarized (in a report) to document the range of responses for a pattern.

Importantly, the documentation process should not be lengthy and cumbersome since patterns should be responded to and resolved rapidly. Any documentation should be realistic and built into the officers' and sergeants' current mechanisms for recording performance.

Pattern Accountability and Assessment

Pattern accountability includes systematically reviewing the progress of responses and evaluating their success. If the highest ranking patrol personnel on shift are responsible for pattern responses, the patrol geographic area commanders (e.g., district captains) are responsible for accountability of pattern responses. That is, they are responsible for making sure their staff have the necessary resources, are implementing responses immediately and appropriately, are coordinating with other divisions, and are documenting their work. They also evaluate the effectiveness of the responses implemented in their geographic area of responsibility and are held accountable by their superiors (i.e., command staff) for doing so.

Ideally, a weekly meeting among patrol commanders and shift supervisors, as well as commanders in support divisions, facilitates the coordination of personnel and resources among the divisions, the monitoring of response implementation, and the evaluation of response effectiveness (i.e., have crimes related to the pattern activity ceased?). Documentation occurs at this meeting to track the ongoing coordination, responses, and results. Similar to significant and repeat incidents, documentation provides an overview (not specific details) of the responses implemented for each pattern. The following is an example based on the bulletin presented in Figure 5 (on page 21) (note that specific dates, times, and duration of directed patrol, FI cards, and offender contacts are not listed in the summary but would be documented using one of the methods noted previously):

Scanning and analysis: As noted in Pattern Bulletin #2010-246, seven residential burglaries of single family homes occurred between October 22–November 3, 2010 during the day (between 0900 and 1620) on weekdays in the area north of Becker Rd and east of Darwin Rd in Beat 31. The property taken is primarily TVs, computers, cash, and jewelry and in all cases, forced entry was made to either front or rear slider/cabana door.

Response: Patrol: Conducted directed patrol and subject vehicle stops in the pattern area on day shift from November 4–11. Criminal investigations: Contact known offenders listed on pattern bulletin, no results. Crime prevention: Conduct reverse 911 call on November 4 to all residents in pattern area. PIO: Notified neighborhood watch of pattern on November 4.

Assessment: No additional residential burglaries have occurred in the pattern area for two weeks. Pattern closed.

Toward the end of the guide, the section on organizational accountability lays out, in more detail, how the Stratified Model's meeting structure facilitates the accountability and evaluation of crime reduction strategies implemented for patterns as well as the other levels.

Long-Term Crime Reduction

To review, a long-term problem is a set of related activity that occurs over several months, seasons, or years that stems from systematic opportunities created by everyday behavior and environment. Problems can consist of common disorder activity and serious criminal activity. The types of problems include problem locations, areas, offenders, victims, products, and compound problems.

Problem Identification

Based on the organization's priorities, the command staff selects which types of problems will be addressed and the analysis that is produced to assist with the selection process. Because problems are manifested over long periods of time, routine identification of problem locations, areas, offenders, etc., use one to three years of data. At least one year should be analyzed to consider the seasonal variations in a particular problem type. The specific type of data used depends on the crime reduction goal and type of problem selected. For example, a goal to reduce disorder at problem locations or street blocks examines specific types of calls that indicate disorder.

Once the type of problem and data have been selected, the problem identification process seeks to prioritize those addresses, areas, people, or products that have been the hardest hit, so resources can be used most efficiently with the largest potential impact. Both research and practice show that crime and disorder do not occur randomly, but cluster in places, areas, by people, etc. An "80/20 analysis" is used to determine a large number of incidents (i.e., 80 percent) that have resulted at or from a few people, places, areas, etc. (i.e., 20 percent). The result of an 80/20 analysis identifies which of the targets (e.g., addresses, blocks,

Rank	Location	Disturbance and Fight Calls	% Calls (N=576)	Cumulative %	% Addresses (N=65)	Cumulative %
1	800 S Darwood Blvd	45	7.81%	7.81%	1.54%	1.54%
2	1449 E Morrow St	44	7.64%	15.45%	1.54%	3.08%
3	1055 S Main St	42	7.29%	22.74%	1.54%	4.62%
4	1675 N West Av	40	6.94%	29.69%	1.54%	6.15%
5	1850 S Gatland Rd	39	6.77%	36.46%	1.54%	7.69%
6	1655 E Walton Rd	32	5.56%	42.01%	1.54%	9.23%
7	166 W Peacock Blvd	25	4.34%	46.35%	1.54%	10.77%
8	973 S Deloir Rd	21	3.65%	50.00%	1.54%	12.31%
9	269 S Foster Av	20	3.47%	53.47%	1.54%	13.85%
10	220 N Irving St	19	3.30%	**56.77%**	1.54%	**15.38%**
	Other Addresses (55)	249	43.23%	100.00%	84.62%	100.00%
	Total	**576**	**100.00%**		**100.00%**	

activity and should be prioritized for response. Table 4 is an example of an 80/20 analysis of problem bars (locations) for general disturbances and fights and lists the top 10 bars in descending order showing that these 10 addresses (15.38 percent of the addresses) account for almost 60 percent (56.77 percent) of the crime. Using this as a scanning tool, some or all of the top locations can be selected for crime reduction and would be further examined before responses are initiated.

To use the 80/20 analysis for different types of problems, there are additional points to consider, including:

Problem locations and areas: This analysis results in a list of the individual locations or areas that account for the most crime, disorder, etc., over a period of time and can be conducted on a range of geographic units, depending on the nature of jurisdiction and the activity being examined. Analysis can be conducted for specific addresses, for locations (i.e., apartment complex with multiple addresses), for types of locations (e.g., intersections, bars, construction sites), for street blocks, and areas. No matter the geographic unit selected, the analysis should focus on specific types of incidents (e.g., street robbery, residential burglary, drug related incidents, disorder calls, traffic crashes).

Problem offenders: This analysis results in a list of offenders who have been arrested by the agency over a period of time along with real-time intelligence of offender's cur-

of crime or types of offenders (e.g., juveniles; individuals living in a particular area). Additionally, offenders' crimes may be weighted to account for seriousness of their crimes. For example, in an analysis, violent crimes might be multiplied by 2, so an offender arrested for 3 robberies (value of 6) is higher than an offender committing 5 theft from vehicles (value of 5).

Problem victims: This analysis results in a list of individuals (e.g., Mary Smith), or types of victims (e.g., female college students) that have been victimized the most over a period of time. The analysis may be limited to specific types of crime (e.g., domestic violence) or, as with problem offenders, types of victimizations can be weighted by seriousness to prioritize victims of more severe crimes.

Problem products: This analysis results in a list of the most frequent types of property stolen over a period of time. It is recommended to use property categories (e.g., jewelry) instead of individual descriptions (e.g., 3.25 carat diamond ring with white gold) of property when conducting the 80/20 analysis. Value of the property taken can also be used to weight the results.

Problem Analysis

Long-term activity requires more in-depth data collection and analysis than repeat incidents and patterns because they are more complex problems. For example, an agency may select the top five bars from Table 4 (on page 26), for which additional analysis is conducted to understand the opportunities that facilitate the problem at each bar and the consequences of the problem activity. There is no one analysis product or set of responses that applies to all types of problems, but there are key questions to which answers are sought during the analysis process in order to understand the local problem and develop tailored, effective responses. They include:[39]

What is the nature of the problem that is occurring? It is important when analyzing a problem to specify the problem in terms of the type of behavior the problem results in (e.g., predatory, consensual) and the type of environment (e.g., residential, retail, public ways) the problem is occurring in. The more specifically a problem is defined, the more focused the analysis and subsequent responses can be. For example, a problem of robbery is too general to analyze and develop responses for in a realistic way; however, a problem of street robbery in commercial districts is more specifically defined and thus focuses the analysis as well as the potential responses.

How frequently is the problem occurring? Frequency can be examined by week, month, season, or annually. Answering this question helps to determine how this problem compares to others and the amount of resources that may be necessary to implement problem-solving responses (e.g., 100 residential burglaries vs. 1,000).

When is the problem happening? According to research, most problematic activity is not distributed equally across time. In other words, activity clusters at certain times of the year (seasonal), days of the week, and times of day. Determining when problematic activity is happening can focus and prioritize crime reduction strategies for that particular problem.

Where is the problem occurring? Similarly to when problems occur, most activity is not distributed equally across geography. Thus, identifying high activity locations or areas for problem activity helps to direct and prioritize crime reduction strategies. Analysis of where the problem is occurring is conducted at multiple scales—from determining which district or precinct has a disproportionate amount of crime to identifying specific places to identifying specific

areas within a single building where the problem predominantly occurs. For example, commercial robberies may occur primarily in one district within a city, drug activity may occur predominantly in one section of a particular park, or assaults in a problem bar may occur primarily around the pool tables.

Who are the offenders, and does repeat offending exist? Similarly to victims, research shows that a small number of offenders account for a large number of crimes, even at the smallest level.[40] Thus, examining who the offenders are and which are repeat offenders can be used to direct and focus problem-solving responses. These may be specific people or a specific demographic (e.g., high school boys).

Who are the victims/targets and does repeat victimization exist? Depending on the type of problem and type of activity, victims or targets will be different. However, it is important to examine who and what the victims/targets are. Research suggests that "lightning does strike twice"—that is, individuals and targets that are victimized once are likely to be victimized again,[41] so identifying repeat victims/ targets *within* each problem helps prioritize and focus problem-solving responses. Conducting additional 80/20 analyses of data from specific locations or areas can further prioritize crime reduction efforts.

Why is the problem occurring? Finally, the critical question is why a particular location, block, area, product, etc., is a problem. The answers to the previous questions along with general research results help to determine the immediate causes. Unfortunately, there is never a way to know the absolute truth about why a problem is occurring, but police can develop thoughtful responses based on research, the answers to these questions, their own experience of the problem and local factors.

In order to answer these questions, the following general process is recommended:

1. Review the research on the problem. The POP Center's *Problem-Specific Guides for Police*[42] are a series in which the research and practice of addressing over 60 problems is published to be used to assist in problem-solving efforts. The guides not only include an overview of the problem type, but also provide suggestions for analysis, assessment, and responses that have and have not worked. Related publications and projects regarding a wide variety of problems can also be found by searching the POP Center website at www.popcenter.org.

2. Examine official data readily available relevant to the particular problem type. Once a problem has been identified through the 80/20 analysis or through other methods, the best place to begin understanding the problem in the local context is in the official data sources available to the agency (e.g., calls for service, crime reports, arrests, etc.).

3. Collect additional data about the problem under examination. Analysis of official police data does not always provide the necessary information to fully understand the causes of a particular problem. Thus, additional data may need to be collected specifically about the problem. Additional data can be collected from people—through interviews, focus groups, and surveys—as well as from places—through environmental surveys and direct observation. This information helps to complete the answers to the questions necessary to begin developing tailored problem-solving responses.

4. Develop response recommendations based on analysis results. Once again, the POP Guides are a valuable tool for developing tailored responses based on the analysis. Crime reduction strategies are chosen based on the results of the analysis, what has worked in other agencies and places, and resources of the agency.

Consequently, in the Stratified Model, as part of the institutionalization of analysis, once a problem has been selected to be addressed, a standardized packet of analysis is automatically provided to the individual responsible for addressing that problem (see discussion of responsibility following this section). Because the packets vary somewhat by problem type, the following is more specific information about what analysis would be provided:

Problem locations and areas

The types of problem locations and areas include, but are not limited, to individual addresses, individual locations with multiple addresses (e.g., apartment complexes), types of locations (e.g., convenience stores), street blocks, and ar-

eas (e.g., neighborhoods). The standardized packet of analysis includes a review of the relevant research and practice on addressing that particular problem, an analysis of call for service, crime, and arrest data, as well as an environmental assessment.

The calls for service analysis includes examination of both citizen and officer generated calls for service data for at least the last 12 months at that location or area. At a minimum, the packet would include a frequency and percent of types of calls, frequency of calls by month or by 4 week period, time of day/day of week analysis for all calls and then selected calls, as well as the frequency and percent of disposition of the calls. The crime and arrest analyses include examination of agency crime and arrest data for at least the last 12 months. At a minimum, the packet would include frequency and percent of crime types and arrest types, frequency of crime and arrests by month or by 4 week period, arrests by age, sex, and race, as well as all relevant crime patterns. The environmental analysis of the problem includes examination of official city information (i.e., zoning, licenses, code enforcement violations, taxes, etc.), background information of owners, occupants, and others (e.g., customers and neighbors), observation of the location/area, Crime Prevention Through Environmental Design (CPTED) evaluation, interviews with officers about the recent activity and history, as well as interviews and surveys with owners, managers, residents, customers, neighbors, etc.

Individual problem offenders and victims

This category refers to individual offenders or individual victims (e.g., John Smith). More often, problem offenders will be examined, but the analysis conducted for offenders often overlaps with the analysis conducted for victims. The standardized packet of analysis of an individual contains much less information than that of a location or area because it is focused on the criminal, victim, and police contact history of only one individual. That is, the packet would include a complete criminal history of the individual from the national database, corrections history and current status, as well as any other contacts made with the police department (e.g., as a victim, a witness, calls for service, traffic citations, etc.). In many cases, associates, residence history, credit history, and history with city services (e.g., utilities, code enforcement) is also included.

Types of offenders and victims

Types of offenders might include college students, gang members, or teenage boys, and types of victims might include taxi drivers, illegal immigrants, and female college students. The standardized packet of analysis includes a review of the relevant research and practice on addressing that particular problem, an analysis of relevant call for service, crime, and arrest data, as well as interviews with individuals who are the offenders, victims, and those that are familiar with the problem (e.g., police officers, social workers, teachers, bar managers).

Products

This category relates to individual products (e.g., IPads, catalytic converters) and types of products (e.g., electronics, car parts) that are targeted over a long period of time. The standardized packet of analysis includes a review of the relevant research and practice on addressing the problem, an analysis of relevant call for service, crime, and arrest data, as well as interviews with offenders, victims, and others that are familiar with the problem (e.g., police officers, retail manufacturers, pawn shops, recycling facilities).

Problem Response

Like analysis, strategies implemented for long-term problems are extremely varied and are specific to the problem and the jurisdictions in which they occur; therefore, they are not covered specifically here.[43] However, as part of the Stratified Model, any strategy implemented for a problem should be documented, so that it can be monitored and evaluated. These are the performance measurements described previously in the goal development section. Some examples of activity that can be tracked for problems include the number of officer contacts, arrests, cleared cases, potential victims contacted, media releases, and crime prevention contacts.

In addition to performance measures, the chronology of strategy implementation should be documented. Specific dates when arrests were made, training programs imple-

mented, and physical changes made to problem locations and areas should be tracked in order to ensure responses are being implemented in a timely manner as well as to evaluate their effectiveness in reducing the problem.

Problem Accountability and Assessment

Because long-term problems are more complex and require a more complex analysis and response, as indicated in the Stratified model, mid- and upper-level managers (e.g., lieutenants and captains) are assigned the responsibility of overseeing long-term crime reduction activities and thus would be provided the crime analysis packet described previously. Although it is likely that the manager will subsequently delegate some aspects of the problem solving process, the manager should be directly involved with analytical and response decisions, as well as ensuring that the work is ongoing and being conducted in a timely manner.

In order to make the workload realistic and to ensure those with the most knowledge of a particular problem are assigned responsibility, problems are broken down by geographic area and by type. The following are general recommendations for the assignment of different types of problems, noting that adjustments would be made depending on the size and organization structure of an individual agency:

Problem locations and areas: Patrol geographic commander (i.e., district or precinct captain).

Problem offenders: Criminal investigations commander—because in most agencies, repeat offender or chronic offender units are housed in this division.

Problem victims: Criminal investigations commander—because in most agencies, victim assistance and domestic violence units are housed in this division.

Problem products: Criminal investigations commander—because in many agencies, pawn units and evidence sections are housed in this division.

Compound problems: Because compound problems are very complex and encompass some or all of the problem types listed previously, it is difficult to assign the responsibility of a compound problem to a particular division commander. Thus, the responsibility of a compound problem would be assigned according to the nature of the problem, the expertise of the commander, and the resources of the agency.

The chief and the command staff would hold commanders accountable for crime reduction strategies implemented for all long-term problem types. Because these problems require long-term responses to resolve the problem, daily and weekly review is not effective or realistic for accountability, but instead, monthly updates should be used to discuss the ongoing progress of the strategies as well as to determine whether they are working. Once a problem is considered completed and resolved a final summary would be prepared from ongoing documentation to provide the highlights of the analysis, response, and overall assessment of the problem. This final summary would not only be used as evidence of the crime reduction work being done, but also as research when similar problems arise in the future. Even problems that are not successfully resolved would be documented in order to learn from mistakes and ineffective responses. Toward the end of the guide, the section on organizational accountability lays out, in more detail, how the Stratified Model's meeting structure facilitates the accountability and evaluation of crime reduction strategies implemented for long-term problem types as well as the other problem levels.

Crime Reduction Evaluation

In addition to implementing strategies for crime reduction, a key component of the Stratified Model, based on the problem solving process, is the ongoing evaluation of crime reduction efforts that focuses on assessing whether all levels of crime reduction strategies are effective in reducing the crime and disorder outlined in the agency's goals. Consequently, where action-oriented analysis and accountability focuses on the responses to each pattern individually and whether a pattern is resolved successfully, evaluation-oriented analysis and accountability seek to assess whether the responses to all patterns are effective over time and whether they are having an impact on the overall levels of crime. Evaluation of crime reduction strategies occurs on a monthly and semi-annual basis since enough time must be

allowed to pass before overall efforts can be reviewed and assessed.

Monthly Evaluation

The purpose of a monthly evaluation is to ensure that all levels of crime reduction efforts are being consistently applied, appear to be working, and seem to be having an overall impact on crime and disorder. A full evaluation of crime reduction efforts is not realistic on a monthly basis, so this monthly evaluation serves to check in on the progress toward the agency goals and hold commanders accountable for crime reduction activities in their divisions. Because crime counts can vary widely from month to month, analysis focuses on identifying trends instead of on numerical differences or percent change from month to month. The following are a series of crime analysis products that are most effective for monitoring crime reduction activities on a monthly basis. Although any one of these products can be formatted differently and can contain different information, the objective here is to provide an example of products and explain their specific purposes in the evaluation process.

Crime and Disorder Trend Chart (Six Months)

Figure 8 on page 31 is a bar chart that is created each month for the *most recent* 6 months compared to the same 6 months of the previous year, with a trend line for each time period and the percent change from one year to the next for all 6 months together. The purpose of this analysis is to assess crime reduction efforts at every level (e.g., immediate to long-term) for one type of activity over the last 6 months in comparison to the same time last year to account for seasonal patterns of crime. Its purpose is not to anticipate future trends, as those are addressed in the semi-annual analysis with a different set of products. One chart would be created for each type of activity identified in the agency's goals as well as by individual geographic areas and citywide, as appropriate.

Although the counts for each month are illustrated by the bars, the interpretation of the chart focuses on the two trend lines and the overall percent change between the two 6-month periods. For example, Figure 8 shows that the most recent 6 months have a downward trend where the

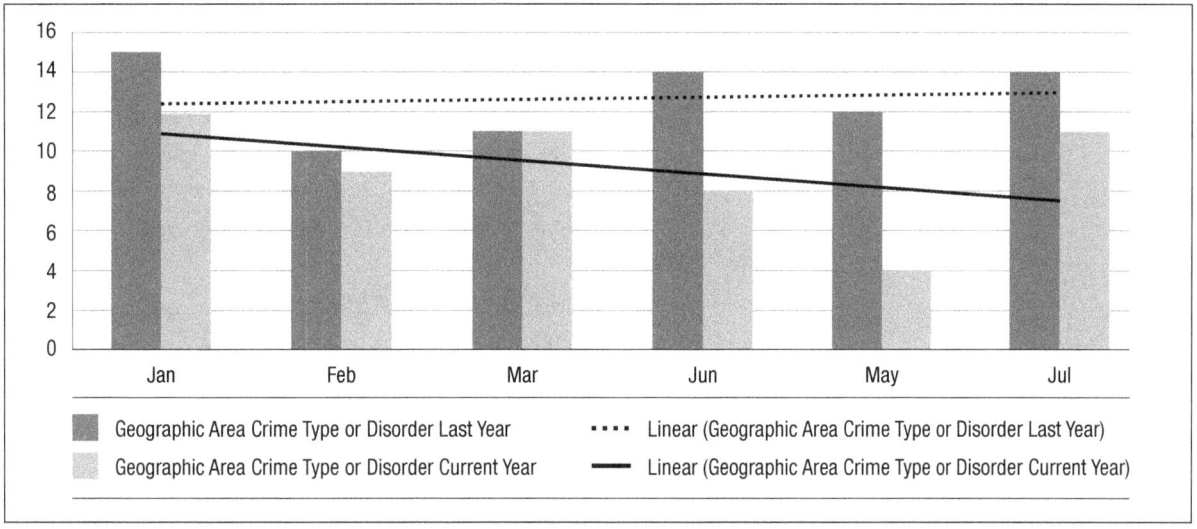

Figure 8: Crime Trend Chart of Crime or Disorder (Six Months)

same months last year show a slight upward trend. Additionally, there is a 28 percent decrease in the total from the last year to the current year. Thus, it appears as though the crime reduction efforts are having an impact on the problem depicted in this chart.

Crime Pattern Trend Map

This analysis product is a static map that is used to determine whether patterns are clustering over time and becoming larger, long-term problems. In order to create the Crime Pattern Trend Map, an agency must be conducting pattern analysis. Figure 9 (on page 32) is a single symbol map depicting only one type of crime at a time (e.g., residential burglary). On the map, incidents or areas that represent where specific patterns have occurred are marked by ellipses that are labeled with the month the pattern was identified. Other information that may be included is the pattern number and whether or not the pattern was resolved. In any case, the type of map (e.g., symbol or density), type of crime, symbology, and the denotation of the patterns (e.g., ellipses or boxes) can vary by agency preferences.

The length of the time period examined in the analysis depends on the number of crime incidents and patterns and the needs of the agency. Because the product is used to monitor short-term crime reduction, the time period should

be no less than 3 months and no more than 12 months. Each month, a new map would be created with data from the *most recent* 3 to 12 months depicting each type of crime identified in the agency's goals as well as by individual geographic areas and citywide.

Although the interpretation of a monthly map may be imprecise, in that it does not definitively show emerging problems on a monthly basis, these maps are examined continually to determine ongoing clusters of patterns that are not resolved. For example, in Figure 9, the map indicates that the southernmost area has recurring patterns. Based on their own judgment, commanders decide to monitor this area over the next several months and/or implement additional strategies.

Individual Problem Chart

Figure 10 (on page 32) is a bar chart depicting ten problem locations that have been selected for long-term crime reduction through an 80/20 analysis and each location's total amount of disorder calls. Each month, a new chart would be created depicting the *most recent* 6 months of activity at these addresses compared to the same 6 months of the previous year. The purpose of the chart is to monitor the impact of the crime reduction strategies at each of the 10 locations individually. Separate charts would be created for

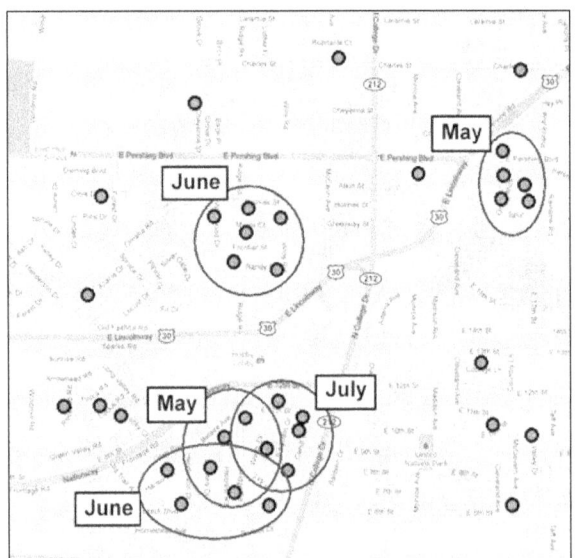

Figure 9: Residential Burglary Pattern Trend Map: May–July

problem locations, disorder calls for service are lower in the current 6 months versus the same months last year (except Locations #3 and #6), and the disorder calls for service have decreased overall by 16 percent at these ten locations. These results indicate that the current strategies seem to be working overall, but that Locations #3 and #6 might require some adjustments or additional response.

Aggregate Problem Trend Chart

Figure 11 on page 33 is a chart that uses the same data as in Figure 10 each month but examines the problem type differently to provide an overview of the agency's efforts over time at all ten locations together. Thus, it reflects the counts for all ten locations by month and compares the *most recent* 6 months to the same 6 months of the previous year with a separate trend line for each time period (similar to Figure 8 on page 31). Separate charts would be created for each of the different types of problems as well as for individual geographic areas and citywide.

As with the Crime and Disorder Trend Chart (Figure 8), the interpretation of Figure 11 focuses on the two trend lines and the overall percent change between the two 6 month periods. It shows that the disorder calls for service from January to June in the previous year for the ten selected

each type of problem (i.e., problem bars, problem violent offenders) as well as for individual geographic areas and citywide, as appropriate.

The interpretation of the chart focuses on the individual locations as well as on the overall percent increase or decrease. For example, Figure 10 shows that for most of the

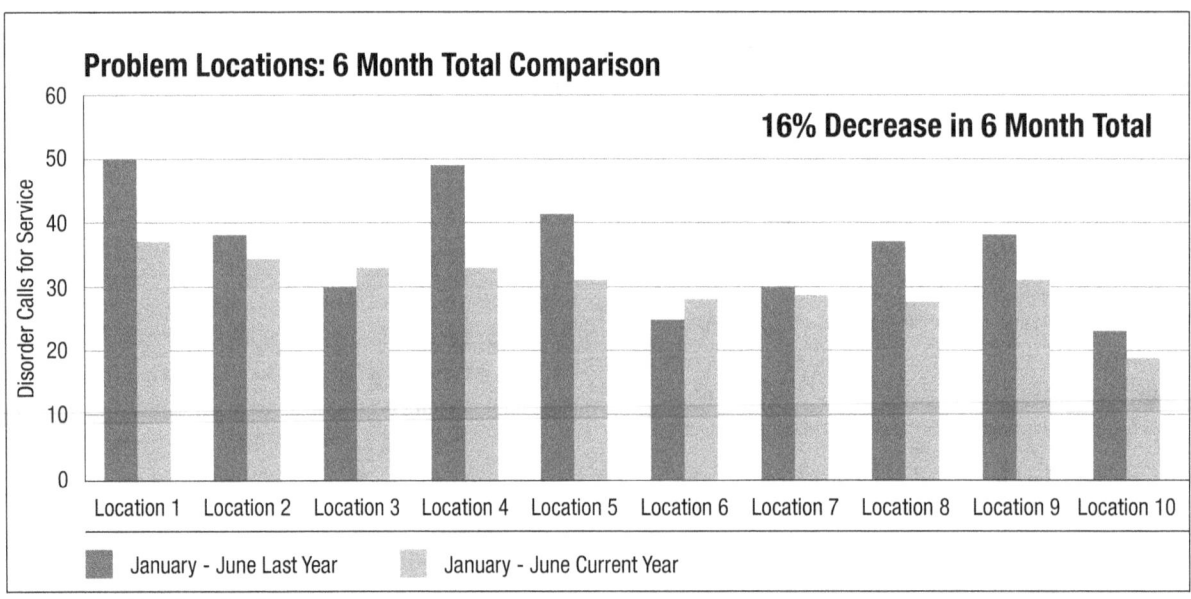

Figure 10: Problem Location Chart

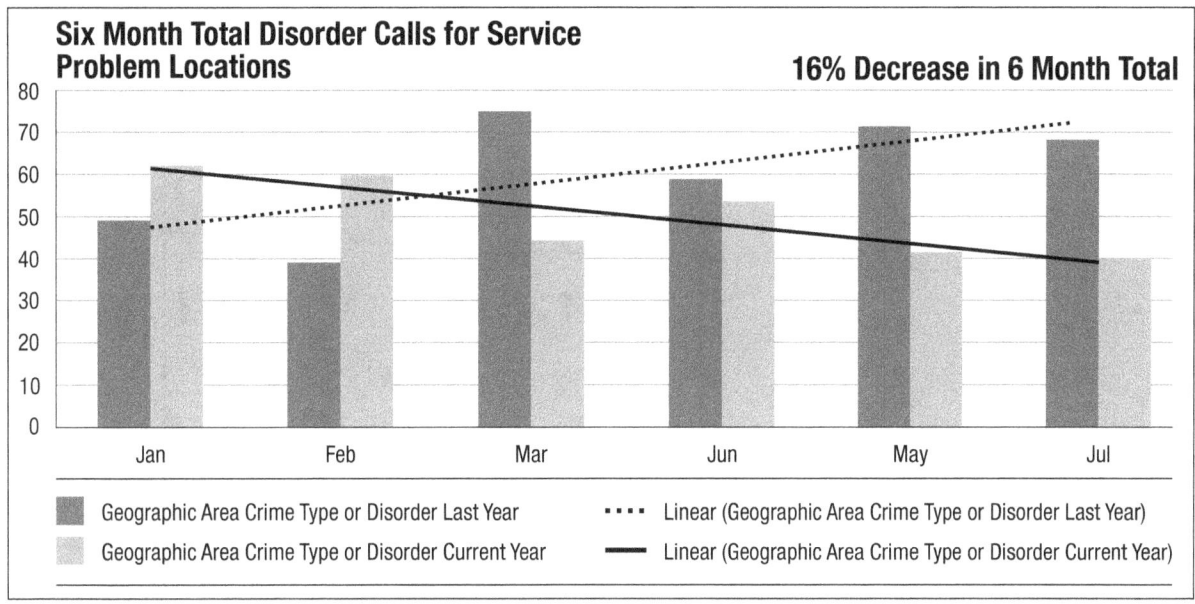

Figure 11: Problem Location Trend Chart

problem locations had a striking upward trend, which is why these locations were selected. Importantly, the trend line for the same months this year shows that there is a downward trend in calls for service and that there is a 16 percent decrease overall, which indicates that the responses may be having an impact.

Semi-Annual and Annual Evaluation

The purpose of a semi-annual evaluation is to assess the implementation of all crime reduction activities and their impact on the agency's established crime reduction goals. Although the procedures here are discussed as if the evaluation occurs every 6 months, agencies may opt to evaluate their problem-solving efforts every 12 months depending on their needs. However, it is recommended that an evaluation of goals occur at least once a year in order to ensure accountability is occurring at every level of crime reduction. The data used for assessment come from a variety of sources and include documentation of crime reduction strategies occurring at every level; operational data on costs of personnel time, equipment, etc., for implementing responses; crime and disorder data from the agency; and comparison data from neighboring jurisdictions, the state, and national sources.

Process Evaluation

There are several types of analysis products that would be created to assess whether crime reduction strategies have been *implemented successfully* and have been *cost effective*. They include both a content analysis of crime reduction activity documentation as well as a cost analysis of the strategies implemented. First, analysis of the documentation of crime reduction strategies is used to assess the success rate of crime reduction efforts at every level in the agency as well as by geographic area. That is, of the activity specifically selected for problem solving, how quickly and effectively were responses implemented? For example, the analysis would examine the number of weeks it took to resolve individual repeat incidents and patterns, the number of responses, which divisions responded, and the coordination of the responses.

Second, a cost analysis would examine the number of the personnel hours (both scheduled and overtime) and other costs required for crime reduction activities at each level (e.g., deployment of bait vehicles, purchase of additional equipment). These cost analyses may be conducted for one agency goal at a time or for all short-term strategies generally (e.g., pattern responses) within the time period of the goal. Although accounting for every cost is difficult, mea-

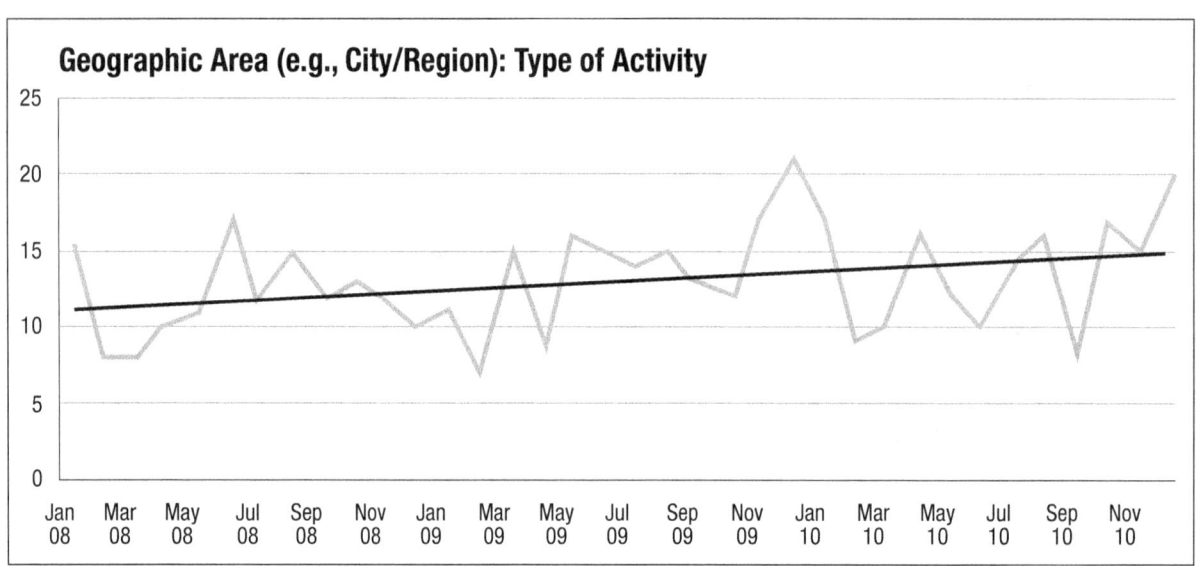

Figure 12: Change in Crime/Disorder Density Map

suring the majority of the costs in a consistent way allows comparisons among different strategies and their impact on organizational resources as well as comparisons over time.

Impact Evaluation

To assess whether short- and long-term strategies are having an impact on the levels of crime and disorder, there are a number of different analysis products that would be created to serve this purpose. Because the Stratified Model and its implementation emphasizes practical processes, instead of recommending highly academic and statistical methods of evaluation, these products focus on data readily available and analyses that are realistic in the context of a police organization.

Crime and Disorder Trend Chart (Three Years)

Figure 12 is a generic line chart that depicts the frequency by month for 3 years of data as well as a trend line for that period. The purpose of this chart is to evaluate the impact of all the agency's strategies for a particular goal. Three years of data are used to see whether the levels of activity are increasing or decreasing beyond the immediate goal assessment period (5 or 12 months) to provide context to the changes. A minimum of 3 years should be analyzed to illustrate any long-term impact, but more data is recommended, when appropriate. Separate charts would be created for

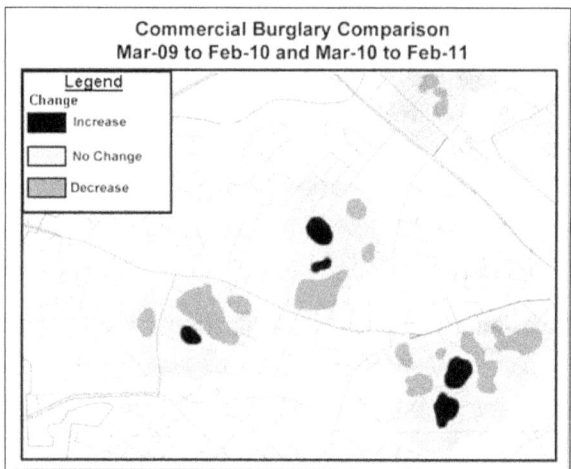

Figure 13: Change in Commercial Burglary Map

each type of crime or other activity identified as an agency goal. Separate charts would also be created for different geographic regions to make comparisons among areas.

Figure 13 is a density map that highlights areas where the activity has increased or decreased from the baseline to the target time period of a particular goal (e.g., commercial burglary). The purpose of the map is to evaluate the long-term hotspots of a particular type of activity to determine where levels have changed. The map may indicate areas of decreased crime levels as well as examine displacement of activity to different areas. The analysis could also be conducted with a graduated area map. Separate maps would be created for each type of crime/disorder addressed in the agency's goals.

Crime Trend Comparison Chart

To assist with determining whether decreases are occurring because of the agency's crime reduction activities and not because of other reasons (e.g., economy, or natural disasters), it is useful to compare crime and disorder changes to those occurring in other similar local jurisdictions. For example, if street robberies have decreased by 20 percent in the agency but only 5–10 percent in neighboring jurisdictions, the agency has more confidence that its crime reduction strategies have made an impact. In addition, line charts illustrating crime per population rate trends can be used to compare an individual jurisdiction to other local jurisdictions, the state, and the nation. For example, in Figure 14, even though the agency's residential burglary rate is higher than the state rate overall, where both the neighboring jurisdiction's and state's rates are increasing the agency's rate is decreasing.

Notably, rate per population is not always the best denominator for comparison for certain types of crime. Unfortunately, it is difficult to get comparison measures from other jurisdictions or state and national levels, so population is often the most realistic and practical comparison measure. It may also be difficult to obtain specific crime (e.g., residential burglaries at apartment complexes) and call for service information (e.g., disorder calls) from other agencies, so these charts may primarily be created by year with more general crime types. Because of these considerations, making conclusions based on more general crime comparisons should be done cautiously.

Annual Identification of Emerging Problems

To anticipate future trends and identify new crime problems on an annual basis, analysis products can also help to look at both long-term trends of crime and disorder not already selected as crime reduction goals as well as new problem types for current goals. To identify emerging problems that may become a new agency goal, two of the analysis products previously discussed are used.

First, the Crime and Disorder Trend Chart (Figure 12 on page 34) is used; however, instead of examining data to assess the agency's stated goals, this chart would be created with data from *potential* crime and disorder problems (i.e., those not already chosen as goals). Secondly, the 80/20 analyses described previously (Table 4 on page 26) can be

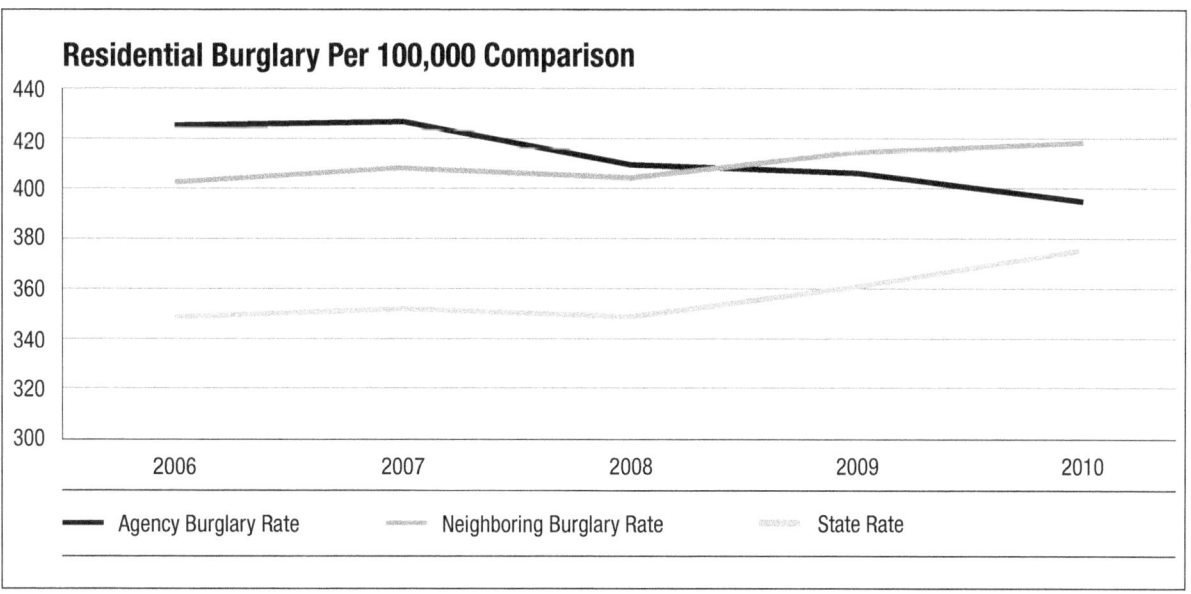

Figure 14: Crime Rate Comparison Chart

used to identify new problem locations, areas, offenders, victims, and property to be selected for response over the next 6 to 12 months.

Lastly, the Seasonal Crime and Disorder Trend Chart is used to help identify emerging problems. Figure 15 is a line chart that depicts frequency by month of a specific type of activity for 3 years, comparing each month to the same month in the previous 2 years. The purpose of this product is to look for seasonal patterns in the crime generally (e.g., residential burglaries that increase over summer months) as well as to identify seasonal trends and times of the year in which to prioritize responses for a particular problem that has already been selected.

Organizational Accountability Structure

The primary objective of the accountability structure within in the Stratified Model is to regularly facilitate the implementation and coordination of and evaluate the appropriateness and effectiveness of crime reduction strategies implemented at each level in the organization. At the immediate level, accountability processes determine whether calls for service and crimes are being responded to and documented

(i.e., report quality) effectively, and whether significant incidents are being afforded the appropriate resources and responded to quickly and effectively.

At the short-term level, they determine if responses to repeat incidents and patterns are coordinated and immediate, are effective, and whether long-term problems are emerging. At the long-term level, the accountability processes help identify problems, ensure responses are implemented, and determine if responses are effective. Finally, at the organizational level, accountability processes determine whether the agency is conducting the problem solving process effectively at all levels and is achieving its crime reduction goals.

As noted in the Stratified Model overview, to facilitate these processes, an accountability structure is necessary and involves a system of meetings that are characterized by their temporal nature, their purpose, and the type of activity they address. By institutionalizing a meeting structure, the attendance of specific individuals at particular meetings is not as important as having someone there who represents a division, unit, or rank, and has the knowledge about the topics discussed, as well as the authority to make decisions involving resources during the meeting.

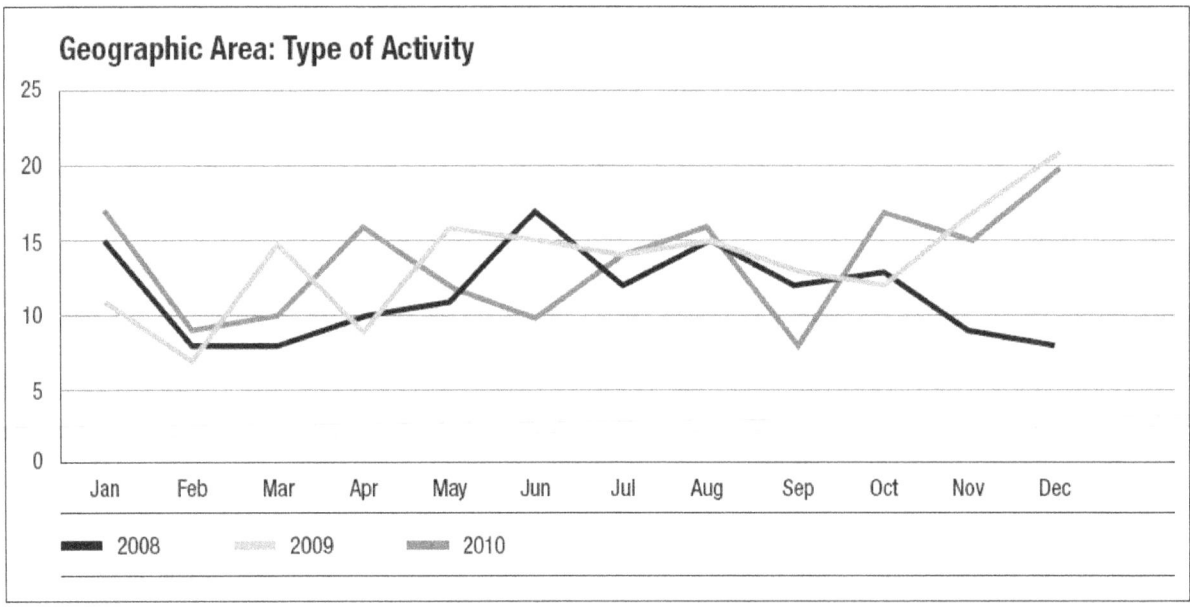

Figure 15: Seasonal Crime and Disorder Trend Chart

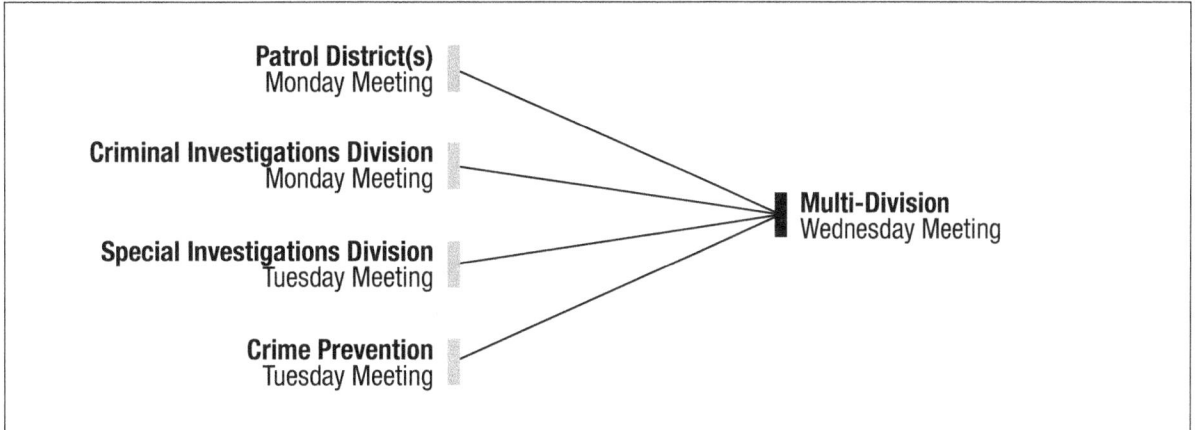

Figure 16: Set of Weekly Meetings

Daily Meetings

There are two types of formal daily meetings that agencies typically hold. However, depending on the size and structure, an agency may develop other ways of communicating and holding people accountable on a daily basis (e.g., electronic briefing). The most important concern here is creating a *system* for communication that is not dependent on any one or two individuals seeing each other, but is institutionalized into the day-to-day operations of the agency. In addition, because daily meetings occur so frequently, it is not realistic to formally document what is discussed in each meeting.

The first type of formal meeting is the line-level roll call, which facilitates *action-oriented* accountability at the line level for crime reduction strategies implemented for immediate and short-term problems. These brief meetings that typically occur at the beginning of patrol shifts are the primary conduit for communicating at the line level 24 hours a day, 7 days a week for all issues in the agency. For immediate activity, these daily meetings are used to ensure data quality, to implement responses to incidents, and to assess the effective implementation of those immediate responses. For short-term problems, daily meetings are used primarily to deploy patrol officers and other specialized units or support personnel (e.g., criminal investigations, crime prevention) for repeat incident and pattern responses for the current shift. First-line supervisors and shift supervisors in patrol and criminal investigations use these daily meetings,

as well as contact in the field, to communicate with officers about this work.

The second type of formal daily meeting is a briefing attended by command staff and upper-level managers, which also facilitates *action-oriented* accountability, but at the command level. Although these briefings can cover activities other than those related to crime reduction, agencies can use them to ensure that significant incidents and patterns are responded to immediately, that collaboration among divisions is occurring, and that the necessary resources are made available (also referred to as "mission based policing").

Weekly Meetings

There are two main types of weekly meetings that can facilitate *action-oriented* accountability for short-term crime reduction in the Stratified Model. Discussion of responses to repeat incidents and patterns would occur in these meetings, and that discussion would be formally documented for accountability and evaluation purposes.

The first type is a meeting attended by personnel within a geographic area (i.e., district) or a division in which a commander holds the respective lieutenants and sergeants accountable for short-term crime reduction. The second type is a meeting attended by personnel from various divisions across the organization who come together to develop, coordinate, and assess these short-term responses. Although this may not be necessary in smaller agencies, a *combination* of action-oriented weekly meetings would be conducted to ensure short-term responses are coordinated, immediate, and relevant to the patterns at hand. Figure 16 (on page 37) depicts an example of how weekly meetings could be held in each of the respective divisions. The days the division meetings are held are provided to indicate that they must be held *before* the multi-division meeting to review division responses that are subsequently discussed in a multi-division weekly meeting.

Monthly Meetings

Monthly meetings facilitate *evaluation-oriented* account-ability within geographic areas and are used to discuss analysis that checks in on the progress of the agency's crime reduction goals. They are used to assess whether short-term problem-solving responses seem effective and whether long-term problems are emerging, as well as to monitor the progress of ongoing long-term problem-solving activities. Consequently, in monthly meetings, the command staff holds geographic and division commanders accountable for the effectiveness of responses to significant incidents, repeat incidents, patterns, and all problem types, as well as for emerging problems stemming from chronic repeat inci-dents and patterns. Documentation of these meetings would consist of the meeting agenda as well as copies of formal presentations made at the meeting.

In *every* monthly meeting, the different division and geo-graphic area commanders make succinct presentations of the crime reduction activities that fall under their command. The presentation of significant incidents, repeat inci-dents, patterns, and problems reflects the collective work conducted by all divisions even though it is made by the commander of one division. However, because individual commanders are responsible for making sure responses are coordinated, implemented, and effective, they are also responsible for making the presentations and answering questions from the command staff. Consequently, com-manders from the other divisions should be prepared to answer questions about their role in supporting patrol in the responses to the repeat incidents and patterns.

Each commander's presentation contains brief summaries of the analysis, response, and results for each level of crime reduction. For each significant incident, repeat incident, and pattern discussed, one to two slides would be used. For long-term problems, multiple slides would be necessary depending on what is being presented; however, the focus should be on brevity and the content should be organized by the analysis, response implementation, and assessment, as relevant.

As commanders present their information, the command staff uses weekly documentation of crime reduction activi-ties to develop questions that ensure the work is being done efficiently and effectively, that collaboration between and among divisions is occurring, and that all necessary resources are provided. Presentations by *patrol area com-manders* would include the following:

■ **Selected repeat incidents:** Because there may be a large number of repeat incident locations addressed each month, the commander would select only those that were addressed successfully since the last meeting in his/her geographic area. Those repeat incidents locations that are still being addressed are not included in the formal presentation, but the commander would be prepared to discuss them if asked. The command staff uses the weekly documentation from weekly meetings to develop questions that ensure repeat incidents have been responded to efficiently and effectively. Note that in smaller agencies with less crime, repeat inci-dents would be a major focus of a commander's presenta-tion whereas in larger agencies with more crime, discussion of repeat incidents may be very short or not included at all. Importantly, the level of accountability for repeat incident problem solving depends on the goals of the agency and the prioritization by the leadership.

■ **Patterns:** The commander presents all patterns that were newly published, actively responded to, or resolved since the last monthly meeting in his/her geographic area. The command staff uses documentation from each pattern or from the weekly meetings and their own knowledge to develop questions that ensure patterns have been responded to efficiently and effectively.

■ **Emerging problems:** The commander presents any long-term problems emerging from repeat incidents and patterns (that could not be resolved and continue to reoccur over time) identified since the last monthly meeting.

■ **Problem locations and areas:** The commander provides a brief update on the progress of any problem locations or areas that have been selected for long-term crime reduction. The amount of information that is presented depends on the status of the problem-solving activities at the time of the meeting. For example, a presentation after completion of the analysis phase would be longer than one conducted during the middle of response implementation, when only a brief update would be necessary. As noted previously, a final presentation of the entire problem-solving process is made after the assessment has been conducted.

Presentations by *criminal investigations* or *special investigation division commanders* would include the following:

■ **Significant incidents:** Because significant incidents typically involve follow up investigations, they are the responsibility of the criminal investigations and/or special investigations division commander. All or some of the significant incidents resolved or responded to since the previous meeting may be selected for presentation, depending on the quantity and the command staff's preference. No matter which significant incidents are presented by the commanders, he/she is prepared to answer questions on any significant incident that has met the agency's criteria and has been addressed that month. Even though significant incidents are considered immediate activity, the investigations can take several months, thus, those significant incident investigations that take a considerable amount of time would be discussed in this forum.

■ **Problem offenders:** Similar to the presentation of problem locations and areas, the commander provides a brief update on the progress of any problem offenders that had been selected for long-term response.

■ **Problem victims:** Similar to the presentation of problem locations and areas, the commander also provides a brief update on the progress of any problem victims that had been selected for long-term response.

■ **Problem products:** Similar to the presentation of problem locations and areas, the commander also provides a brief update on the progress of any problem products that had been selected for long-term response.

Following the commanders' presentations, the crime analyst or the command staff (if there are no crime analysts) would present the evaluation products discussed earlier to help the command staff assess whether short-term problems are becoming long-term problems and *monitor* the effectiveness of both the short-term and long-term problem-solving responses. It may appear as though it takes a significant amount of time in a meeting to discuss this material; however, this meeting occurs monthly, not weekly, and each agency prioritizes the information to be presented according to its goals, needs, and resources as well as the time they are willing to spend. In the agencies that have implemented the model, these meetings typically take between 1 to 3 hours each month.

Semi-Annual Meetings

Semi-annual meetings facilitate evaluation-oriented accountability for the entire organization and its goals. They are used to examine long-term trends to determine the effectiveness of the agency's crime reduction approaches at all levels, to identify new long-term problems to be addressed over the next 6 months or more, as well as to formulate new agency goals and strategies for the coming year(s). The command staff holds themselves and their subordinates accountable for the long-term impact of the entire agency's crime reduction activities.

In the semi-annual (or annual) meetings, the agency leader and the command staff use analysis results to make conclusions about the effectiveness of all problem-solving responses implemented by the agency and to determine whether the agency's goals have been achieved. This process requires careful consideration, as the conclusions are not based simply on statistics, but are also based on agency resources, the community climate, and comparisons to other jurisdictions. However, unlike the monthly meeting, division commanders would not present in these meetings. The analysis product and evaluation results would be presented by those that have conducted the analysis (e.g., crime analysts for crime data; budget managers for cost analysis) and the command staff themselves.

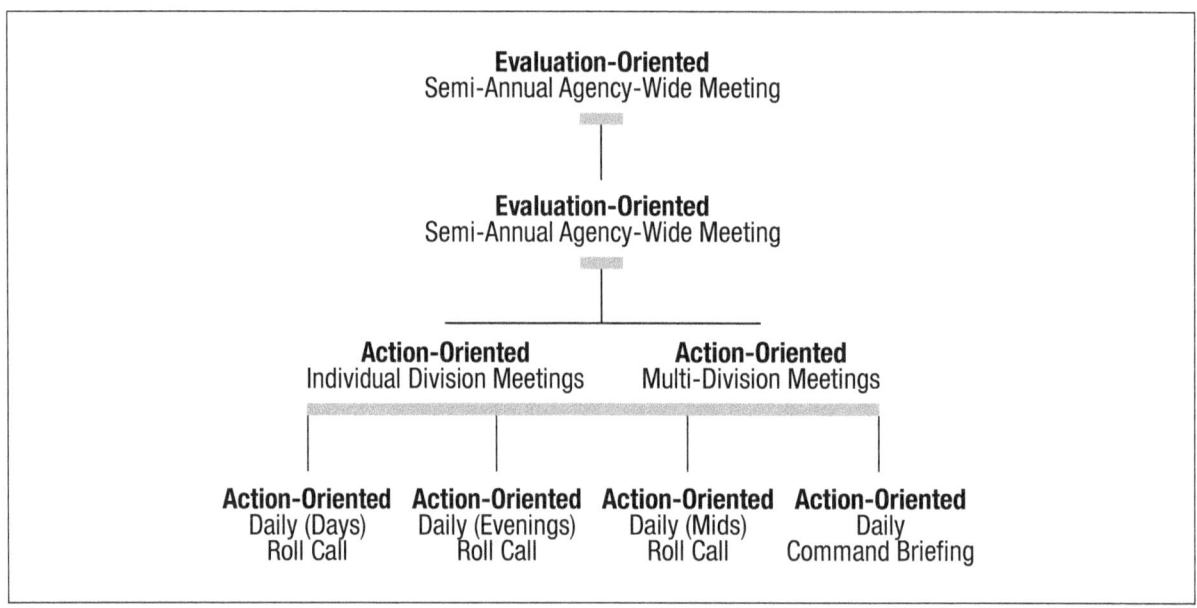

Evaluation-Oriented
Semi-Annual Agency-Wide Meeting

Evaluation-Oriented
Semi-Annual Agency-Wide Meeting

Action-Oriented
Individual Division Meetings

Action-Oriented
Multi-Division Meetings

Action-Oriented
Daily (Days)
Roll Call

Action-Oriented
Daily (Evenings)
Roll Call

Action-Oriented
Daily (Mids)
Roll Call

Action-Oriented
Daily
Command Briefing

Figure 17: Stratified Meeting Structure

The meetings typically take between 1 and 3 hours depending on the size of the agency and the amount of information discussed. In some cases, agencies may treat the meetings as staff retreats and reserve an entire day to discuss the analysis, goals, and other organizational concerns. Ultimately, the goal of the these meetings is for the command staff to determine whether 1) to continue with the goals and same crime reduction strategies, 2) make adjustments to the current goals and strategies, or 3) identify and implement new goals and strategies.

Stratified Meeting Structure

Within the stratified approach of the model, these meetings create a formal system of accountability and evaluation which is *stratified* to match the complexity of the problems addressed and the rank of those primarily responsible for implementing crime reduction strategies. Figure 17 illustrates the relationship of the individual meeting types, how they can feed information about responses and effectiveness to one another, and ultimately create a system of accountability for the agency.

Tailoring the Stratified Model

To adapt and tailor the model to a particular agency's organizational structure, this section presents an overview of the general rank assignments that are recommended for the Stratified Model and a succinct view of the model's structure (Table 5 on page 41).

First-line supervisor: Typically a sergeant, but may also be a corporal. In very small agencies, this could be a captain or lieutenant if they do not have sergeants.

Patrol shift supervisor: Highest rank working the midnight shift for the entire city or area. Because all ranks work during the day shift (e.g., business hours), to determine the rank of the patrol shift supervisor across all shifts, look to the midnight shift. In larger agencies, this is a lieutenant; in smaller agencies, a sergeant. Officers are not supervisors, so cannot serve in this position. When tailoring the model to a particular agency, responsibility is assigned a higher rank rather than a lower one. If there is no supervisor on evenings or midnight shifts, this reverts to a patrol supervisor working day shift (primarily applicable in small agencies).

Patrol area commander: The Stratified Model works best for agencies whose structure assigns patrol commanders responsibility by geographic area. Thus, this is the rank

Table 5: Overview of the Stratified Model Implementation

Problem Complexity	Data Used for Analysis	Analysis Products	Assigned Response	Assigned Accountability	Accountability Meeting Frequency/ Documentation
Incidents	1. Calls for service 2. Crime	Police training	Officers and detectives	First-line supervisor	Daily roll calls/ Calls for service, Crime reports
Significant Incidents	Crime selected by specific criteria	Daily report	Detectives and their supervisors	Criminal investigations manager and commander	Weekly/ Incident summaries
Repeat Incidents	Calls for service	Weekly report	Patrol first-line supervisor	One rank above	Weekly/ Meeting minutes
Patterns	Crime	Crime pattern bulletin	Patrol shift supervisor	One rank above	Weekly/ Meeting minutes, Pattern response summary
Problem Locations and Areas	1. Calls for service 2. Crime	1. 80/20 analysis 2. In depth analysis for each location or area	Patrol area commander	Bureau commander	Monthly/ Meeting presentations
Problem Offenders	1. Arrest data 2. Criminal history	1. 80/20 analysis 2. In depth analysis for each offender	Criminal investigations commander	Bureau commander	Monthly/ Meeting presentations
Problem Victims	Crime	1. 80/20 analysis 2. Follow up analysis on each victim	Criminal investigations commander	Bureau commander	Monthly/ Meeting presentations
Problem Products	Property	1. 80/20 analysis 2. Follow up analysis on each property type	Criminal investigations commander	Bureau commander	Monthly/ Meeting presentations
Compound Problems	Varies	Varies	Selected commander	Command staff	Monthly/ Meeting presentations
Agency Goals	1. Police data 2. Population 3. Meeting minutes 4. Cost	1. Three year trend charts and map 2. Meeting minutes analysis 3. Cost analysis	Entire agency	Chief and Command staff	Semi-annual/ Meeting presentations

responsible for an entire area (multiple shifts). In larger agencies, this is a captain; in smaller agencies, this could be a lieutenant or sergeant.

Criminal investigations division manager: This rank is responsible for managing all or part of the criminal investigations division. Oftentimes, this rank is equivalent to a patrol shift supervisor (e.g., lieutenant or sergeant).

Criminal investigations division commander: This rank is responsible for all of the criminal investigations division.

Oftentimes, this rank is equivalent to a patrol area commander.

Special operations division commander: The rank that is responsible for various specialty units (e.g., narcotics, gangs, homeland security). Oftentimes, this rank is equivalent to a patrol area commander.

Patrol bureau commander: The rank that supervises all patrol area commanders and is in charge of the entire patrol function (may have other units as well). In larger agencies, a major or deputy chief; in smaller agencies, a captain or lieutenant; in the smallest agencies, could be the chief.

Support services bureau commander: The rank that supervises criminal investigations and/or a combination of other support divisions. In larger agencies, major or deputy chief; in smaller agencies, captain or lieutenant; in the smallest agencies, could be the chief.

Command staff: The chief and the next level of commanders below the chief. These ranks vary by size of agency (e.g., large agencies: majors, lt. colonels; medium: captains, majors; small: lieutenants, sergeants). These individuals are typically the bureau commanders.

Resources and Considerations

A question for any police leader looking to implement the Stratified Model is "What organizational changes and resources are necessary to be successful?" Because the Stratified Model seeks to infuse systematic crime reduction strategies into the existing structure of the agency, few, if any, significant organizational changes need to be made in most agencies. However, problem-solving skills and knowledge, improvements in data, development of processes, and crime analysis capabilities are all areas in which a leader may have to direct attention and resources toward, to effectively implement the model. The following is a brief discussion of each consideration and a list of additional resources to carry out the model.

Data

In order to create a system for crime reduction, all relevant police data should also be systematized. It is not absolutely necessary to have a computerized data system to implement the model, but it does make the entire process easier and more realistic to accomplish. However, even those with computerized police report writing programs and records management systems may need to improve both the content of the data and how it is collected before the model can be implemented effectively. Most importantly, data collection and data quality must become a high priority to the leadership of the agency and is paramount in successfully implementing all or parts of the Stratified Model.

Training

In order to implement the Stratified Model, all personnel should be educated in the Stratified Model and its implementation into a specific agency, as the application of problem-solving techniques, crime opportunity theory, documentation processes, and the accountability meetings will vary by the size and scope of the organization. Training would be provided to all ranks—that would include the framework of the Stratified Model and the problem solving process as well as examples of crime analysis products, crime reduction strategies, and accountability responsibilities relevant to that agency. Separate training would be conducted for line officers and detectives, sergeants, and managers (lieutenants and captains) to focus on their roles in the process specifically, as appropriate. One of the purposes of this guidebook is to serve as the foundation for the necessary education and training of department personnel.[46]

Crime Analysis Capacity and Placement in the Organization

The Stratified Model cannot be effectively implemented without designated personnel assigned to conduct crime analysis. Crime analysis must be conducted consistently and effectively, as the entire model depends on analysis products that are systematically produced. Because crime analysis requires a significant amount of time and specialized skills, it is necessary to have at least one full-time crime analyst. Depending on the size of the agency, multiple analysts could be necessary. The standard recommendation within the industry is one analyst for every 100 police officers;[47] however, additional analysts may be needed depending on the breadth and scope of an agency's implementation of the model.

Another important consideration for crime analysis is the placement of the crime analysis function in the organizational structure of the agency. Once an agency begins to systematically use analysis to enact crime reduction strategies and hold personnel responsible for these activities, the crime analysts become vulnerable to undue influence by commanding officers who may seek to manage their own workload and success. For this reason, it is recommended to house the crime analysis function in an "accountability-neutral" division, where it is supervised by personnel outside the accountability structure for crime reduction activities (e.g., an administrative bureau). The crime analysts will, of course, provide products for patrol, criminal investigations, and other operational divisions, but their priorities must be set by supervision outside the operational structure and accountable to the chief of police.

Process Development

As part of the foundation of implementing the Stratified Model, a set of analysis, problem solving, and accountability processes and policies must be developed that are tailored according to an agency's own current policies and procedures. The guidebook presents examples for these processes and techniques to serve as a starting point. When developing these processes, input should be sought from all ranks of the agency, especially for those processes that directly affect that rank either through the crime reduction strategies or the accountability structure. Notably, this work should be done before agency training is conducted so that personnel are trained on the exact processes they will be held accountable for. It is recommended to create general orders and guidelines for these processes and procedures as this is how practices become institutionalized and prioritized into the day to day business of the police agency.

Resources

Finally, there are numerous resources available from the COPS Office through the Center for Problem-Oriented Policing (*www.popcenter.org*) that can assist in the training and implementation of the problem solving process and crime analysis. They include:

Problem-specific guides: *The Problem-Specific Guide Series* summarize knowledge about how police can reduce the harm caused by specific crime and disorder problems. These are individual guides to prevention and to improving the overall response to incidents, not to investigating

offenses or handling specific incidents. These guides have drawn on research findings and police practices in the United States, the United Kingdom, Canada, Australia, New Zealand, the Netherlands, and Scandinavia. Each guide is informed by a thorough review of the research literature and reported police practice and is anonymously peer-reviewed by line police officers, police executives, and researchers prior to publication.

Response guides: *The Response Guide Series* summarizes the collective knowledge from research and practice about how, and under what conditions, certain common police responses to crime and disorder do and do not work.

Crime analysis guide: *Crime Analysis for Problem Solvers: In 60 Small Steps* (2005) is a practical guide for police and analysts that provides direction in theory and specific analytical techniques.

References

Barthe, E. (2006). *Crime prevention publicity campaigns.* Washington D.C.: U.S. Department of Justice, Office of Community Oriented Policing Services.

Bernasco, W. (2010). A sentimental journey to crime: Effects of residential history on crime location choice. *Criminology,* 48: 389–416.

Boba, R. (2010). A practice-based evidence approach in Florida. *Police Practice and Research* 11: 122–128.

Boba, R. (2009). *Crime analysis with crime mapping, Second edition.* Thousand Oaks, CA: Sage.

Boba, R. and J. Crank. (2008). Institutionalizing problem-oriented policing: Rethinking problem identification, analysis, and accountability. *Police Practice and Research* 9: 379–393.

Bowers, K., and S. Johnson. (2003). *The role of publicity in crime prevention: Findings from the Reducing Burglary Initiative.* (Home Office Research Study No. 272.) London: Home Office.

Braga, A. (2008). *Crime prevention research review No.2: Police enforcement strategies to prevent crime in hot spot areas.* Washington, D.C.: U.S. Department of Justice, Office of Community Oriented Policing Services.

Brantingham, P. L., and P. J. Brantingham. (1993). Nodes, paths and edges: Considerations on the complexity of crime and the physical environment. *Journal of Environmental Psychology* 13(1): 3–28.

Clarke, R. V. (1999). *Hot products: Understanding, anticipating and reducing demand for stolen goods* (Paper No. 112, Police Research Series). London: British Home Office Research Publications.

Clarke, R. and J. Eck. (2005). *Crime analysis for problem solvers: In 60 small steps.* Washington D.C.: U.S. Department of Justice, Office of Community Oriented Policing Services.

Cordner, G., and E. P. Biebel. (2005). *Problem-oriented policing in practice. Criminology & Public Policy* 4: 155–181.

Crank, J., D. M. Irlbeck, R. Murray, and M. Sundermeirer. (2011). *Mission based policing.* New York, NY: Taylor & Francis.

Eck, J., S. Chainey, J. Cameron, M. Leitner, and R. Wilson. (2005). *Mapping crime: Understanding hot spots.* Washington D.C.: U.S. Department of Justice, National Institute of Justice.

Eck, J., R. Clarke, and R. Guerette. (2007). *Risky facilities: Crime concentration in homogeneous sets of establishments and facilities.* Edited by G. Farrell, K. Bowers, S. Johnson, and M. Townsley, *Imagination for Crime Prevention: Essays in Honour of Ken Pease, Crime Prevention Studies* (Volume 21). 225-264.

Felson, M. and R. Boba. (2010). *Crime and everyday life* (Fourth Edition). Thousand Oaks, CA: Sage Publications.

Goldstein, H. (2003) On further developing problem-oriented policing: The most critical need, the major impediments, and a proposal. *Problem-oriented policing: From innovation to mainstream.* Monsey, NY: Criminal Justice Press.

IACA [International Association of Crime Analysts] (2011). International Association of Crime Analysts (IACA). www.iaca net.

IACA [International Association of Crime Analysts]. (2011). *Crime pattern definitions for tactical analysis* (White Paper 2011-01). Overland Park, KS: Author.

IACP [International Association of Chiefs of Police] (2010). *IACP/Sprint Excellence in Law Enforcement Research Award Program: Spotlighting the Power & Impact of Law Enforcement Academic Research Partnerships.* Alexandria, VA: IACP.

Newman, G. (2007). *Sting operations.* Washington D.C.: U.S. Department of Justice, Office of Community Oriented Policing Services.

Santos, R. (2011). *Systematic pattern response strategy: Protecting the beehive*. FBI Law Enforcement Bulletin, (February): 12–20.

Scott, M. (2000). *Problem-oriented policing: Reflections on the first 20 years*. Washington, D.C.: U.S. Department of Justice, Office of Community Oriented Policing Services.

Scott, M. (2004). *The benefits and consequences of police crackdowns*. Washington D.C.: U.S. Department of Justice, Office of Community Oriented Policing Services.

University of Maryland (2011). *Institutionalizing CompStat in the State of Maryland*. www.compstat.umd.edu.

Weisburd, D. (2005). Hot spots policing experiments and criminal justice research: Lessons from the field. *The Annals of the American Academy of Political and Social Science* 599: 220–245.

Weisburd, D. and J. Eck. (2004). What can police do to reduce crime, disorder and fear?" *The annals of the American academy of political and social science* 593: 42–65.

Weisburd, D. L. and A. Braga. (2006). *Police innovation: Contrasting perspectives*. Cambridge, UK: Cambridge University Press.

Weisburd, D., S. D. Mastrofski, A. McNally, R. Greenspan, and J. J. Willis. (2003). *Reforming to preserve: Compstat and strategic problem solving in American policing, Criminology and Public Policy* 2: 421–456.

Weisel, D. L. (2005). *Analyzing repeat victimization*. Washington D.C.: U.S. Department of Justice, Office of Community Oriented Policing Services.

Author Biographies

Rachel Boba

Dr. Rachel Boba is an associate professor at Florida Atlantic University in Boca Raton, Florida and has been working with police for over 17 years. Before moving to Florida, she was a Senior Research Associate and Director of the Crime Mapping Laboratory at the Police Foundation in Washington, D.C. where she carried out large-level research projects that focused on crime mapping, crime analysis, and problem-oriented policing. Her current publications and research focus on institutionalizing crime reduction strategies into the daily routine of police agencies through the implementation of analysis and accountability. In addition to implementing her Stratified Model of Problem Solving, Analysis, and Accountability into the Port St. Lucie, Florida Police Department, she has assisted other agencies in adopting the model and has trained agencies throughout the United States and worldwide. Two of her recent books include one sole-authored; *Crime Analysis with Crime Mapping, 2nd Edition* (2009), and the other co-authored with Professor Marcus Felson; *Crime and Everyday Life, 4th Edition* (2010). She earned her M.A. and Ph.D. in Sociology from Arizona State University.

Roberto Santos

Detective Lieutenant Roberto Santos has been with the Port St. Lucie, Florida Police Department for over 17 years. Currently, he oversees the daily operations of the criminal investigations division which includes persons, property, and financial crime, the crime scene investigators, the narcotics and gang units, as well as the crime and intelligence analysis unit. Det. Lt. Santos has been the catalyst for creating a department-wide system for institutionalizing crime analysis, crime reduction strategies, and accountability for tactical and strategic problems in the Port St. Lucie Police Department. He has assisted law enforcement agencies and trained police personnel around the United States in institutionalizing crime analysis, crime reduction strategies, and accountability as well as has sole-authored and co-authored several published articles on this topic. He is a graduate of the FBI's National Academy, earned his Masters in Criminology and Criminal Justice at Florida Atlantic University, and has been an adjunct professor for FAU since 2006, teaching upper division criminology and criminal justice classes.

Endnotes

1 Weisburd and Eck (2004); Weisburd and Braga (2006).

2 Cordner and Bibel (2005); Goldstein (2003); Scott (2000); Weisburd and Braga (2006).

3 Boba and Crank (2008).

4 Weisburd, Mastrofski, McNally, Greenspan, and Willis (2003).

5 Boba and Crank (2008).

6 Boba (2010).

7 The PSLPD is located on the east coast of Florida around 120 miles north of Miami. Its population in 2011 is around 160,000 and covers 114 square miles. As of November 2010, over 220 officers have been authorized for the agency. The city is mostly made up primarily of single family homes and the Part I crime rate averages around 2,900 per 100,000.

8 The agencies include, but are not limited to, the Campaign, IL, Cincinnati, OH, Dayton, OH, Ft. Pierce, FL, and the Anne Arundel County, MD Police Departments as well as other agencies throughout the State of Maryland (University of Maryland, 2010).

9 IACP (2010).

10 Boba and Crank (2009).

11 Information about the Stratified Model based on Boba and Crank (2008) but enhanced through current practice-based research.

12 See www.popcenter.org for more about the SARA process.

13 Boba (2009).

14 Eck, Clarke, Guerette (2007).

15 Braga (2008); Eck, Chainey, Cameron, Leitner, and Wilson (2005); Weisburd (2005).

16 See www.popcenter.org/glossary.

17 Weisel (2005).

18 Clarke (1999).

19 See Boba (2009), Chapter 5 for details about how data should be improved for analysis purposed.

20 Boba (2009).

21 In the largest agencies, specific units may be assigned to deal with very specific types of repeat incidents, such as a traffic unit or a domestic violence unit assigned to focus on their specialties. Agencies with a large contingency of community policing officers may assign the responsibility of addressing general repeat incident locations to this unit where the community policing supervisors would be responsible for selecting locations and overseeing analysis and responses with the officers conducting most of the hands on work.

22 Boba (2009).

23 See Boba (2009), Chapters 8-11 for additional information on data used for pattern analysis as well as for pattern analysis methodology.

24 IACA (2011).

25 See Boba (2009), Chapter 11 for components of a pattern bulletin.

26 Santos (2011).

27 Weisburd and Braga (2006).

28 Adapted from Boba (2009).

29 For more information on both directed patrol and field contacts, see the Center for Problem-Oriented Policing response guide, *The Benefits and Consequences of Police Crackdowns* (2004).

30 For more information, see the POP Center response guide, *Sting Operations* (2007).

31 Ibid.

32 Bernasco (2010); Brantingham and Brantingham (1993).

33 Bowers and Johnson (2003).

34 For more information about contacting victims directly, see the POP Center response guide, Crime Prevention Publicity Campaigns (2006).

35 Ibid.

36 Santos (2011).

37 Felson and Boba (2010).

38 For specific instruction on how to conduct an 80/20 analysis, see Clarke and Eck (2005, Step 18) and Boba (2009), Chapter 14.

39 See also Boba (2009), Chapters 13 and 14 and/or Clark and Eck (2005) for detailed descriptions of the analysis techniques and considerations for examining each question.

40 Felson and Boba (2010).

41 Weisel (2005).

42   Can be found at www.popcenter.org.

43 See the Problem Solving Guide Series as well as the Response Guide Series produced by the POP Center at www.popcenter.org.

44 See Boba (2009), Chapter 12 for a more detailed discussion of using rates for comparison.

45 Crank, Irlbeck, Murray, and Sundermeirer (2011).

46 See also www.compstat.umd.edu which details a project in which a system of training is being conducted to implement the Stratified Model in agencies across the state of Maryland.

47 IACA (2011).

A Police Organizational Model for Crime Reduction: Institutionalizing Problem Solving, Analysis, and Accountability presents a new and comprehensive organizational model for the institutionalization of effective crime reduction strategies into police agencies, called the Stratified Model of Problem Solving, Analysis, and Accountability. It describes all the components of the Stratified Model in a succinct and practical way to provide police managers and commanders with a template for improving the efficiency, effectiveness, and accountability of their agency's crime reduction efforts. Although the objective is to implement all aspects of the Stratified Model, an agency may choose to implement parts of the model as needed or to implement the model in phases.

U.S. Department of Justice
Office of Community Oriented Policing Services
145 N Street, N.E.
Washington, DC 20530

To obtain details on COPS Office programs,
call the COPS Office Response Center at 800.421.6770

Visit COPS Online at www.cops.usdoj.gov